Town&Country

HANDBOOK
FOR HOSTS

*A Practical Guide to Party Planning
and Gracious Entertaining*

Town&Country

HANDBOOK
FOR HOSTS

*A Practical Guide to Party Planning
and Gracious Entertaining*

ADAM BLUESTEIN
ILLUSTRATIONS BY JOSÉ LUIS MERINO

HEARST BOOKS
A Division of Sterling Publishing Co., Inc.
New York

Copyright © 2006 by Hearst Communications, Inc.

Special thanks for their invaluable assistance to David Feldstein of Atherton Wine Imports; David Chianese of Social Expressions in Providence, Rhode Island; Sunny Halperin and Gary Halperin of Party Rental Ltd.; and Alan Bell at David Ziff Cooking.

Monopoly is a registered trademark of Hasbro. Scrabble is a registered trademark. All intellectual property rights in and to the game are owned in the U.S.A. and Canada by Hasbro Inc., and throughout the rest of the world by J.W. Spear & Sons Limited of Maidenhead, Berkshire, England, a subsidiary of Mattel Inc. Mattel and Spear are not affiliated with Hasbro. Trivial Pursuit is a registered trademark of Horn Abbot Ltd. and Horn Abbot International Ltd. Pictionary is a trademark of Pictionary, Inc.

Library of Congress Cataloging-in-Publication Data
Bluestein, J. Adam.
  Handbook for hosts : a practical guide to party planning and gracious entertaining / from the editors of Town & Country ; text by J. Adam Bluestein ; illustrations by José Luis Merino.
     p. cm.
  Includes bibliographical references and index.
  ISBN-13: 978-1-58816-554-1
  ISBN-10: 1-58816-554-X
  1. Entertaining. 2. Parties. I. Town & country (New York, N.Y.) II. Title.
  TX731.B575 2006
  642'.4—dc22

                                                     2006006664

10 9 8 7 6 5 4 3 2 1

Design by Celia Fuller.

Published by Hearst Books
A Division of Sterling Publishing Co., Inc.
387 Park Avenue South, New York, NY 10016

www.townandcountrymag.com

For information about custom editions, special sales, premium and corporate purchases, please contact Sterling Special Sales Department at 800-805-5489 or specialsales@sterlingpub.com.

Distributed in Canada by Sterling Publishing
c/o Canadian Manda Group, 165 Dufferin Street
Toronto, Ontario, Canada M6K 3H6

Distributed in Australia by Capricorn Link (Australia) Pty. Ltd.
P.O. Box 704, Windsor, NSW 2756 Australia

Manufactured in China

Sterling ISBN 13: 978-1-58816-554-1
      ISBN 10: 1-58816-554-X

CONTENTS

FOREWORD

The job of a host can be many wonderful things, but there is one thing it surely isn't—easy. Don't let anyone tell you otherwise. (And never ever buy books called *Easy Entertaining* or *Entertaining in Fifteen Minutes* because they are making false promises.) I've entertained almost all of my adult life—at home, in restaurants, with and without caterers, under tents, in the rain, in spaces large and small. No matter how few people you invite, the moment the list adds up to eight people or more, you will have work to do. This is not to say that being a host can't be fun and gratifying and stimulating (ideally, all of the above). But to do it right and in order to get the results you want—i.e., a good time had by all—it helps to be organized. Scratch that, it is *imperative*.

I've seen parties fall apart simply because the place cards weren't on the table when the guests were ready to be seated. If the cocktail *hour* lasts for ninety minutes, your happy little group may turn grumpy. Wilting flowers will be noticed. Lighted candles in the wrong place can be hazardous. Heaven forbid if the food arrives lukewarm. And on and on.

I recently attended a birthday party at which almost everything that could go wrong did. The place cards were unreadable unless you carried a magnifying glass. And it was a large enough group that there should have been a check-in list to begin with, so people would know which table to head for. The birthday boy—he turned fifty—kept talking to the person next to him as one of his dearest friends tried to give him a heartfelt toast. In total exasperation, the friend abbreviated what he intended to say. Then the birthday boy stood up and read a long excerpt from a book he thought was funny (but nobody else did). It was all downhill from there.

Parties are about details: time, place, attire, choice of food, the mix of people, having enough coat hangers, being at the ready to take drink orders and knowing when it's time for guests to leave. A good host— and for purposes of this book, we are using the word to designate either a man or a woman—is also sensitive. She's keeping an eye out for anything that might go wrong; he's rescuing a guest from being monopolized or another who seems to be all by her lonely self in a corner. Being a host means being on the job. It may be your party; however, you are anything but the guest of honor. Your role is to put everyone at ease. Making introductions is your responsibility. Deciding when guests should be seated is your call. Same for when dessert is served. If you like being in control, then being a host is for you. If you don't, content yourself with being a partygoer, not a party giver.

Suppose you are not only the host but are also doing the cooking. Then plan it so that you don't prepare something that needs a lot of last-minute attention. My own rule is pretty simple: I will happily cook for under ten guests and my ideal group is six to eight people. If it's more than this, I hire someone to help serve and clean up. If I want to be sure to be available to my guests at an event involving twelve or more guests, I will usually hire a caterer. And even then, there are plenty of details to be worked out.

Here's where *Town & Country's Handbook for Hosts* comes in. I can't promise it will reduce a complicated situation into something simple, but I hope it will, at the very least, offer some good advice and pave the way to having a memorable event.

No matter how many parties I've given as editor in chief of *Town & Country* and in the years preceding, and no matter how many times I say, "Never again!" at the end, entertaining, especially at home, remains one of the most gratifying ways to give pleasure to your friends and family, to bring people together in an intimate setting and to spend the kind of time with them that couldn't be spent otherwise. But just remember the advice of another famous handbook (that of the Boy Scouts)—"Be Prepared."

—Pamela Fiori, Editor in Chief
Town & Country

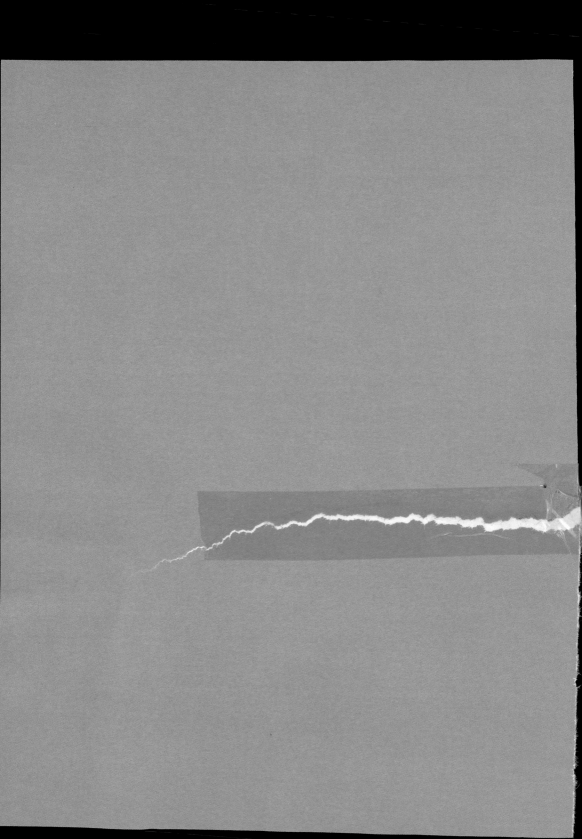

INTRODUCTION

This is not a book about how to be a perfect host or even a proper one. Oh sure, it is filled with rules and guidelines and everything you could ever want to know about the right way to write an invitation, make an introduction, mix a martini and serve a meal. But if you're worrying about dotting every *i* and crossing every *t*, you risk missing the big picture: Parties should be fun.

Yes, entertaining can also be hard work; that's what keeps party planners and caterers in business, after all. And a little bit of host anxiety is probably inevitable and not a bad thing if it keeps you on your toes. But if the very thought of entertaining has you on edge, take a deep breath and reevaluate. Remember, there are as many ways to have a party as there are people. Start small, be informal and above all, be yourself.

You don't need to plan an elaborate meal, set a perfect table or spend lots of money. If you are warm, relaxed and gracious, you will be a successful host. If you're at your ease, your guests will be, too. The secret to being at ease, of course, is being prepared. That's where this book comes in. Use it as you see fit: for information, inspiration or simple reassurance. Read it from cover to cover or keep it on hand for quick reference. If it helps you feel a little more prepared or a little more confident—wonderful. If it makes you want to have a party just for the fun of it, so much the better.

PART I

Party Preparations

WHAT TYPE OF EVENT?

The point of a party, above all, is to have fun. This goes for you, the host, as well as your guests. Don't plan an event so ambitious that pulling it off leaves you so stressed that you're unable to enjoy it yourself.

The first question you need to ask when planning a party is *Why?* What's the purpose of your gathering? To bring together a small group of good friends, to expand your social circle, to celebrate the special achievement of a friend or family member or to mark a significant milestone, like a birthday or anniversary? Once you've defined the *why* of your party, it will be much easier to work out the *who*, *what*, *when* and *where*.

Like snowflakes, no two parties are exactly alike. But when it comes down to it, most parties fall into one of three major categories: cocktail party, dinner party or buffet. What follows are some guidelines to help figure out which major category best describes your next party. Whichever format you choose, make sure always to have a definite timeline in mind—when guests should arrive, when you'll serve dinner, and when, ideally, you'd like them to leave. If you hire a caterer, be sure to discuss the timeline with her.

Cocktail Party

How many? As a rule of thumb, a party should be either small enough so everyone can sit or big enough so those who are standing won't feel awkward. For a cocktail party where people will be standing and sitting, professional party planners use 4 to 5 square feet per person as a guide. Count available space only; subtract the room taken up by large pieces of furniture that can't be moved.

What you need: Table for a bar (with a tablecloth); liquor and mixers, wine, beer and nonalcoholic drinks; ice (lots of it); glassware and bar tools; and a living room or other large area.

Type of food: Usually hors d'oeuvres only, which can be as simple or elaborate as you like.

Start/end time: Cocktail parties usually last for about two hours, starting at 5 or 6 P.M. Cocktail buffets, where more food is served and guests therefore don't have to worry about their dinner, can start as late as 7 P.M. and last three hours or more.

Dinner Party

How many? Ten at most for a sit-down dinner that you're cooking and serving yourself. (For a larger dinner, consider having a buffet, hiring a caterer or hosting your dinner at a restaurant. Or divide your guest list and host two separate parties!) Table size is a factor also. Too much space between guests makes conversation uncomfortable, so it's okay for dinner-party seating to be on the cozy side. Spacing of about 2 feet from plate center to plate center is ideal. Before sending out invitations, take stock of your plates, serving platters, silverware, glassware and chairs. Do you have enough for the number of people you're inviting?

What you need: Food and wine; light hors d'oeuvres (some bowls of nuts and olives are enough; predinner cocktails are optional); place settings and glassware; table linens; and flowers.

Start/end time: Invite guests to arrive between 7 and 8 P.M. If you're serving predinner cocktails, plan to have dinner ready no more than an hour after guests arrive. Dinner parties usually last three hours or more.

Buffet

How many? Since much of the preparation can be done well in advance and the food service is less labor-intensive than for a sit-down meal, buffets are great for a crowd. But you do want to make sure that all your guests have someplace to sit with their plates of food: a chair, a sofa or outside, weather permitting.

What you need: Wine, beer and nonalcoholic drinks (cocktails are optional); an assortment of make-ahead food that will taste good at room temperature, unless you have hot plates or chafing dishes and professional help to man them; serving platters, plates, silverware and glassware; and a large table for the food and a smaller table for drinks, both with tablecloths.

Start/end time: It depends on the type of party—you can serve brunch, lunch or dinner buffet-style. Evening cocktail buffets typically last from 6 to 9 P.M., and most daytime buffets usually last about three hours, too.

Note: A buffet setup is ideal for a holiday or housewarming open-house party. Since the flow of guests will be staggered, you can invite more people than you would for a traditional buffet.

Making Your Guest List

Once you've decided what kind of party you're having, it's time to draw up the guest list.

A small, sit-down dinner requires the most thought, as you'll all be together for quite awhile, elbow to elbow, with no hope of escape until the coffee is served. A table full of brilliant talkers may seem like a good idea, but make sure to throw in some good listeners, unless an evening of high-volume one-upmanship is what you're looking for.

Your guest list should include not only people who are interesting to you but people who will be interesting to one another, too. This doesn't mean you should assemble a homogenous group, though; inviting people of different ages and professions, both married and single, creates energy and encourages people to talk and to find connections beyond the obvious. But don't invite just one single to a small dinner of all couples, as you don't want a guest to feel like the odd man or woman out. Make sure to always include a few key guests who can be counted on to be talkative, entertaining and unfailingly pleasant. They'll be your deputies in drawing out the quieter guests and keeping the conversation flowing.

For a larger cocktail party or buffet you can take more risks with your guest list and mix things up a bit. Invite people you know well in addition to those you'd like to know better. A diverse crowd makes for an interesting party.

PREPARING YOUR HOME

Now that you have a plan for your party, you'll need to make a plan for your home as well. Start with the big picture. If you need to move any large pieces of furniture before your party, make sure to line up the heavy-lifting help you need in advance. Clean up all the areas your guests will see, and remove anything that adds needless clutter or is too valuable or delicate to risk with guests. That said, you don't

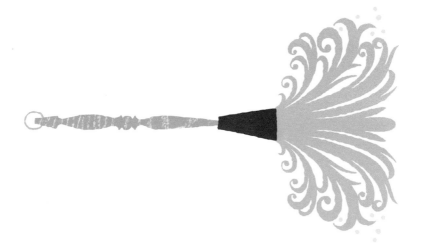

want to strip your home of personality. Displaying family photos, travel souvenirs and a few well-chosen objets d'art helps create a warm, inviting atmosphere where guests feel truly comfortable.

Outside

The welcome you extend to your guests begins even before they enter your home. Make it easy to find your house by making sure your doorstep and front walk are well lit and swept with your address clearly visible from the street.

NICE TOUCH
If it's raining, put some umbrellas (preferably large ones) by the door so you can shuttle guests to their waiting car or taxi dry and safe.

Around the holidays, decorate your front door with a festive wreath or oversize bow. At any time of year, strings of white lights adorning the columns or railing or rows of lanterns lining the walkway will instantly tell your guests that they're in the right place.

Give some thought, too, to where guests will park. If there's not enough room in your driveway or in front of your house, let the neighbors know that your guests will be parking on the street. Not only is it polite, but they may even offer the use of their driveways.

Entryway

When guests enter your home, you want them to immediately see where to put their things. Consider putting a coatrack right in the hallway or entrance. Coatracks and hangers can often be rented from

PARTIES IN APARTMENTS

There's really no space too small to entertain at least a few friends. Just plan the right kind of party and prepare your apartment accordingly:

- If you have a small kitchen, keep your menu simple.
- Serving food buffet style gives you more flexible seating options, since you can move the dining table out of the way to make room for more people.
- Clear all the clutter from the rooms guests will enter, including putting your kitchen appliances away.
- Create more floor space for cocktail-party mingling by pushing the furniture against the walls.
- Strategically place mirrors to make the space seem larger.
- Create some relaxed seating in your bedroom by covering your bed with fabric and adding throw pillows.
- Encourage guests to use any outside space you have. Provide seating and small tables and use candles or other mood lighting to make the outside as attractive as the inside.
- Hire a bartender. Having a professional in charge of the bar ensures that the drink service will be handled smoothly and swiftly, especially important in a smaller space.

party rental companies. Or you can make room in your front hall closet by clearing out your coats and gathering empty hangers (no wire, please!) from around the house for guests' coats. At a big party, try to avoid piling all the guests' coats on a bed as searching for a buried coat is time-consuming and bothersome. If you're working with a caterer, consider requesting that one or two waitstaff help out with the coats at the beginning and end of your event.

Music and Lighting

Music and lighting set the mood for a party as they are the first things your guests will be aware of when they enter your home, so don't underestimate their impact.

A silent room feels lonely and unwelcoming, especially for early party arrivals, so make sure to press the play button before your first guest steps in the door. Adjust your music selections to suit the mood of the party or the different phases of a longer event (upbeat but not conversation-drowning during cocktails and more serene selections for dinner). Unless you want to play DJ all night—or hire one—use your CD player's shuffle feature or program your MP3 player (iPod) with a night's worth of music. (For music suggestions, see page 136.)

Lighting for a party should be soft and flattering. Turn off bright overheads (or soften them with a dimmer) and use floor lamps, sconces and chandeliers instead. "Downlighting" flower arrangements with a small, bright light on a stand lends a dramatic effect. If you have a fireplace, put it to use for fall and winter gatherings. And stock up on candles; their flickering light lends an intimate glow to any space. Cluster small tea-light votives on a table near your entryway and scatter more small clusters around the house to spread the warm light. Groupings of different-size pillar candles are also dramatic and effective. Place candles near reflective surfaces, such as mirrors and windows (without curtains), where their glow will be doubled. Experiment with placing tea lights inside different kinds of glass containers or floating them in water. As a rule, the more candles the better. Just use common sense with their placement and don't put them where they're likely to be jostled or knocked over by guests. For a theatrical presentation of food on a buffet table, use "high-low lighting," with candelabras and candlesticks shining light above the food, and low clustered votives and tiny battery-powered spotlights tucked between the displays of food below.

Temperature

Don't overlook the role of temperature in creating a comfortable environment. Although your living room may feel fine when you're sitting in there by yourself, when you add thirty or forty people, the mercury rises. The more bodies, the more heat, so especially in hot weather, don't invite more people than your space can handle. Turn the thermostat down a few degrees lower than normal or boost the air-conditioning before your party, then monitor the temperature as the house fills up. As people drink and eat spicy foods, they tend to feel even warmer.

Flowers

Nothing says festive like flowers. And you don't need a whole greenhouse-full to make a big impression. Even if you have no knack for making pretty arrangements, clusters of any single flower—tulips, roses or lilies—matched with simple glass or ceramic vases make an elegant statement. Use what's in season or any personal favorites. As an alternative to flowers, consider small potted plants or herbs in decorative ceramic pots.

The Bathroom

Make sure the bathroom your guests use is as clean and uncluttered as the rest of your home. Before the party, clear away personal items, including toothbrushes, contact-lens solution and prescription bottles. And put out a fresh bar of soap and hand towels for guests (with extras out of the way but in sight). As a finishing touch, light a scented candle and dim the lights.

SETTING THE TABLE

The way you set the table sets the tone for the entire meal. Guests notice and appreciate when their host makes an effort to create a pleasant and attractive setting. Your tabletop décor should use colors, textures and materials that complement one another and are tied together by a unifying theme.

Linens, China, Silver and Glassware

The traditional rules say that a tablecloth on a dinner table should fall no more than 15 to 18 inches below the table edge: exactly 18 inches for formal meals, where the cloth will be white damask or linen. As a practical matter, though, tablecloth length is often dictated by the table itself—the metal legs of a rental table, for instance, are not attractive, and so a longer tablecloth that hangs to the floor is sometimes used. And some people simply prefer the draped look of a longer, floor-length cloth. A foam-lined silence cloth is often placed beneath the tablecloth not only to protect the tabletop, but also because it creates a quieter and more luxurious-feeling table. The table is set with linen napkins and matching silverware, china and glassware. Linens should be lightly pressed without creases; silver should be polished; and glassware should be sparking clean and free of water stains and dust (use a buffing cloth after washing).

More relaxed occasions leave more room for creativity. Some hosts enjoy mixing linen patterns and colors and combining different sets of china and glassware. Just make sure the diverse elements create a pleasing whole—you want your guests to think creative, not careless. In lieu of a tablecloth, however, you can use place mats for

PARTIES AT THE KENNEDY WHITE HOUSE

President John F. Kennedy and his wife, Jacqueline Bouvier, were famously sophisticated White House hosts. A typical evening of entertaining would have Jack and Jackie hosting a dinner for eight: a group of close friends along with a writer or artist brought in as a "new face" for the occasion. Italian songs softly played on a record player in the background, and the conversation was informal and candid, ranging from frank discussions of pressing diplomatic issues to equally frank gossip about foreign aristocrats and Kennedy's political rivals.

The Kennedys also gave memorable private dinner dances where waiters carried large trays filled with such exotic mixed drinks as the Cuba Libre, a combination of rum, Coke and lime juice. Their state dinners set new standards for culinary excellence and, for the first time in the White House, featured menus written in French.

The cultural entertainment in the Kennedy White House included classical music and modern ballet performances, as well as Shakespearean drama. The Kennedys also brought together the leading minds in diverse fields, from history to philosophy to ecology, to provoke "great thoughts" for a select group of friends and administration officials.

At once fun-loving and serious, gracious and unguarded, the first couple's vibrant personalities came through clearly in the way they entertained.

a more homey feeling. Before the meal the napkins can be placed, folded, either on top of each guest's empty dinner plate (the formal preference), to the left of the forks, above the plate, on the bread plate or tucked into the wineglass at each place setting. (For more on the exact placement of silverware, glassware and plates, see page 118.)

Note: Save your paper products for outdoor parties. When you invite people into your home, they deserve the best.

Candles and Centerpieces

A centerpiece is another way to show your creativity, but it should never overwhelm the table and get in the way of the food or the guests. Centerpieces should be low enough to see over and not hinder

 the serving or eating of the meal. Flowers are always appropriate as a centerpiece (keep them low, though, so that guests can see over them), as are arrangements of seasonal produce or bowls of fresh fruit. You might also experiment with incorporating natural elements, such as branches, moss, leaves and stones.

For formal dinners, set candles in matching candlesticks or in candelabra placed on either side of the centerpiece. Candlesticks should burn higher or lower than the eye level of seated guests. In a room with other lighting sources, two to four candles are enough for a table of eight. For informal occasions feel free to mix and match the candlesticks or to make clusters of votives or pillar candles. Choose colors that match your tablecloth or place mats, if you like. As with your centerpiece, make sure that candles on the table enhance the atmosphere without being intrusive. For this reason, avoid scented candles; they will interfere with the aromas of the food. And remember, candles should only be used for dinner, not lunch, when the extra light is unnecessary.

Place Cards

When you have eight or more coming for dinner, place cards simplify the seating and make conversation easier, too. Help your guests remember each other's names by writing the names on the front and back of upright place cards or by laying one-sided place cards flat on the table. This makes it possible to read the name of the person sitting right next to you as well as the person sitting on the other side of the table.

The general rules for introductions (see page 53) apply to what you write on place cards. At parties where people don't know each other, use first and last names. At formal dinners, place cards traditionally include each person's title (Mr., Ms., Dr., etc.) and surname only; first names are used if there are two Mrs. Johnsons, for example. While place cards aren't necessary for informal dinners among friends, you can use them to break up old familiar seating patterns. In this case, first names will suffice.

The most formal place cards are made of thick white stock and are sold at stationery stores. The names may be handwritten in black ink or written by a calligrapher. Less formal place cards can be made from any kind of letter paper or card stock you have on hand or just about anything else that can be printed or written on, including postcards, playing cards, photographs or tags or ribbons tied to a small gift for each guest. Elegantly or whimsically designed place cards generated on a computer are also appropriate. Set them directly on the table above the forks, lean them against the glasses or put them on top of the folded napkins on the plates.

Menu Cards

Menu cards, de rigueur at formal dinners, can help elevate even a simple meal into something memorable. Menus are nice because they let guests know what's coming, and they can plan their eating accordingly. Someone may choose to forgo seconds on the main course if she knows she should leave room for the blueberry cobbler dessert.

Menus can be handwritten (in black ink for formal occasions), printed with a computer or done by a calligrapher. If you don't have the wherewithal (or time) to make a menu for every plate, one menu for every two guests is enough. Put the date of the dinner and the reason for having it—Tom and Helen's Anniversary—at the top of the card and encourage your guests to keep their menu cards as a souvenir of the evening.

FOOD AND BEVERAGES

Whether it's the main event or a mere accompaniment, good party food doesn't just happen. The following are some planning tips for hors d'oeuvres, buffets and seated dinners to ensure they will be enjoyed by everyone, including you.

Hors d'oeuvres

The most important thing to remember when planning hors d'oeuvres is that your guests will already have a drink and napkin in their hands, so don't make things harder than necessary. Opt for hors d'oeuvres that can be easily picked up and eaten with your fingers in one or two bites. Keep your guests' clothing in mind, too; avoid any foods with drippy sauces.

For a cocktail party when no meal will be served, be generous with the hors d'oeuvres. Chances are your guests will eat more than you think, especially if the weather is cool. When hosting a dinner party, though, you might forgo elaborate hors d'oeuvres altogether, only offering bowls of nuts and olives. If you do serve hors d'oeuvres before dinner, don't overdo them as the meal is the main attraction, and you don't want your guests to fill up beforehand.

Remember, hors d'oeuvres don't need to be fancy. And don't worry about serving nutritious food either (although you should always include at least one vegetarian option). Think crispy, crunchy, salty and cheesy. Some simple and perennially popular options include:

> Tiny open-face sandwiches
> Hot cheese puffs
> Bite-size crab cakes
> Miniature quiches or pizzas (buy them frozen)
> Miniature puff pastries
> Miniature quesadillas
> Stuffed mushrooms
> Crudités with dip
> Tiny tomatoes filled with goat cheese

Although many people don't think of sweets as cocktail-party food, some hosts like to offer a couple of sweet bites at the end of a party. They perk guests up and send a subtle signal that things are drawing to a close.

Buffets

For a buffet, you'll want to prepare a little more food than you would for a seated dinner, since guests tend to eat more when they're serving themselves. The more selections you make available, the less of each people will eat. For a typical buffet for twenty-five or thirty, your menu might include two large casseroles or a casserole plus a meat dish (sliced ham, turkey and roast beef are good choices); two large salads (or a salad and a cooked vegetable dish); bread or rolls; and two to three desserts. (See the Appendix for tips on figuring the exact amounts.) As you plan your menu, also consider the following:

- Remember that part of the appeal of a buffet meal is saving yourself some work. For that reason, look for dishes that can be prepared well in advance and can be served at room temperature.
- Serve food that won't lose its appeal as it sits. Avoid any dishes that may congeal, shrink or change color.
- Consider sticking to a theme—Middle Eastern (hummus, stuffed grape leaves and sliced pitas), or Italian (antipasto plates and pasta dishes), for example—which helps ensure that all your food looks and tastes good together.
- Since all the courses are grouped on a single plate, which will be carried around by each guest, keep away from wet foods that may run or anything likely to slip off a plate.

CHAMPAGNE AND COGNAC

Think of Champagne and cognac as the beverage bookends of your dinner party. Champagne makes any gathering feel more celebratory. Consider serving it in flutes as guests arrive or serve it during dinner. Champagne is one of the most versatile wines, whether it's dry, extra-dry or brut (the driest and most popular variety). Champagne pairs well with almost any food, including seafood; risotto or pasta with cream-based sauces; spicy Asian dishes and sushi; and dark or bittersweet chocolate.

Bad Champagne can be very bad, indeed, so buy the best you can afford. But don't limit yourself to imported French Champagne only. There are excellent California sparkling wines, as well as the Italian sparkling wine Prosecco, another delicious and even less expensive Champagne alternative.

Cognac and other after-dinner drinks should be offered while guests are having coffee, which may be served either at the dinner table or in a different room. If you are serving after-dinner drinks in your living room, place the bottle or bottles on a tray with the appropriate glassware in a central location, and invite guests to help themselves. At the dinner table, however, pour the drinks for your guests. Serve cognac, armagnac, and brandy in brandy snifters, port in wineglasses, and liqueurs in small, stemmed cordial glasses.

poultry and seafood as well as light pasta dishes and salads. Full-bodied reds, such as cabernet and merlot, pair well with rich foods like beef, lamb and pasta with hearty sauce. There's lots of room for variation, however. Lighter red wines, like pinot noir, work well with certain kinds of seafood, especially salmon, and some white wines stand up quite well to lighter meat dishes. Bear in mind also that some people like to stick with either red or white wine throughout a meal, regardless of what is being served. If in doubt about what to serve, ask your wine seller for guidance; cookbooks and food magazines also offer creative wine-pairing suggestions.

How much wine do you need? An average 750-milliliter bottle yields roughly six 4-ounce glasses of wine; 4 ounces of wine will fill a typical wineglass about halfway, leaving enough room to swirl the wine and enjoy its nose. For a dinner party of average drinkers a half bottle per guest (three glasses) is a safe estimate. Keep an extra bottle or two of white wine chilling in the refrigerator, though, and an extra red unopened on the sideboard. Obviously, if you're serving a drawn-out, multicourse meal or hosting a party of hearty drinkers, buy more wine. (For more on serving wine, see page 80.)

Liquor

There's a saying that good liquor isn't cheap and cheap liquor isn't good. Stock your bar with the highest-quality liquor you can afford and don't hide the bottles. It's not snobbery; it's a way of showing your guests that you think they deserve the good stuff. If offering a full bar (see page 126 for suggestions on stocking a bar) is too pricy or labor-intensive for you, consider serving only wine, Champagne, beer and perhaps a signature cocktail that you can mix up in large

THE PERFECT MARTINI

What precisely constitutes the perfect martini has long been a subject of debate, sober and otherwise. Whether it's made with vodka or gin, a splash or a bucket of vermouth or shaken or stirred, a good martini is always very, very cold. Keep the vodka or gin in the freezer until it's needed, and chill your martini glasses either in the freezer or by filling them with ice (cracked or crushed is best) and letting them sit for a few minutes or until the glass has a frosted look.

This recipe, on the dry side, should please most palates.

INGREDIENTS

2 ounces gin or vodka

$1/4$ to $1/2$ ounce dry vermouth

Pitted green olive or lemon twist for garnish

1. Chill a martini glass.

2. Fill a cocktail shaker about halfway with ice, preferably cracked. Add the gin or vodka and vermouth and shake vigorously. Or fill a large glass tumbler with ice cubes, pour in the gin and vermouth and stir well with a long-handled metal spoon.

3. Strain into the chilled martini glass and garnish with an olive or lemon twist. (Adding a cocktail onion makes the drink a Gibson.)

Makes 1 drink.

batches before the party (martinis or margaritas, for example). Don't forget the nondrinkers. Their beverage options should be just as attractive. Offering a choice of sparkling water, soft drinks, fruit juice, iced tea and perhaps a virgin variation on your signature cocktail is a generous gesture toward those who choose not to drink, and it may encourage everyone else not to overindulge.

If you do offer a full bar, consider tending it yourself (or delegating the task to your spouse or to a friend) rather than letting guests have a go at it themselves. Putting a person in charge usually makes for a neater, more efficient bar area and better drinks. If you plan to offer a full bar for fifteen guests or more, think about hiring a bartender (see page 42). For large cocktail parties, if you have the space, split your bar supplies in half and create two bar areas for quicker drink service. If you opt for a self-serve bar, don't assume it will be self-cleaning. Regularly refresh the ice and napkin supply and make sure to wipe up any spills.

If you'll be tending the bar yourself, consider buying a good bartending manual and stick to the recipes. Assembling a few basic bar accessories will help you mix drinks like a pro:

- A jigger for accurate measurement of liquor quantities
- A long metal bar spoon for measuring teaspoons of sugar and stirring cocktails (Use a glass or plastic stirring rod for drinks with seltzer.)
- A cocktail shaker or a mixing glass with a top and pouring spout (Having one of each will let you easily switch off between shaken and stirred drinks.)
- A muddler for mashing sugar, citrus fruits, mint and bitters
- A bottle opener and corkscrew
- A paring knife and/or citrus zester for anything "with a twist"

- Two ice buckets: one for crushed ice and one for cubes; ice tongs
- Coasters or cocktail napkins, plus bar towels for wiping up

Make sure to have plenty of ice on hand. Buy fresh bags of ice, rather than relying on the stuff from your freezer, which may taste stale or odd. Stock up with more than you think you need as nothing puts the fizzle on a good party like a sudden shortage of ice. Keep the bags out of sight in the kitchen and refill your back-of-bar ice buckets as necessary. Pre-chill glasses for martinis and the like, either in the freezer or by filling them with crushed ice and water. If you're serving wine, put the whites in the refrigerator or in ice buckets well before party time and about a half hour before your guests arrive, uncork a couple bottles each of white and red to prepare for your first guests.

The right glass makes the drink. Few hosts are likely to have all the glassware needed to serve every kind of cocktail in just the right vessel. If you're planning to offer a full bar, you might want to rent extra glassware to ensure that the well-made drinks you're serving get the polished presentation they deserve. (See Rentals, page 43.) With the following lineup, you'll be ready for nearly anything:

- Cone-shaped stemmed cocktail glasses for martinis, cosmopolitans and Manhattans
- Tall, straight-sided highball or collins glasses for most mixed drinks
- Heavy-bottomed old-fashioned glasses for whisky, straight up, on the rocks or a short drink like a gimlet
- Wineglasses for reds, whites and fruit-based cocktails
- Champagne flutes, an elegant touch for any kind of sparkling wine
- Plastic cups for entertaining outdoors

GETTING HELP
WORKING WITH CATERERS
AND BARTENDERS

Caterers

Cooking, serving and cleaning up after a crowd is no doubt some-one's idea of fun. For the rest of us, there are caterers. Working with a caterer is a great way to ease the burden of entertaining while still having a hand in the creative aspects of party planning—and even getting to eat at your own party. While hiring a caterer for a party at your home is typically a bit more expensive than hosting guests at a restaurant, you get more control over the menu, the décor and the cost of items like alcohol, which hosts often purchase themselves for catered events.

To find a caterer, it's best to start with referrals from friends. If you're impressed by the food at a party you're attending, call your host the next day, thank her for a lovely evening and ask who did the catering. If you don't have a particular caterer in mind, meet and get estimates from at least two or three. Ask to see photos of meals they've catered or, better yet, arrange for a tasting. Get the phone numbers of references and call them. Make sure that any caterer you're considering is properly licensed and has the necessary permits and up-to-date insurance.

Before meeting with caterers, work out the details of your event: the date, time, place, type of party (cocktail, buffet or sit-down dinner); the number of guests; the timeline you have in mind and how much you want to spend. Give some thought to the type of food you want, too. Caterers say that their ideal clients are those who are flexible but also have strong ideas of their own. They don't just say, *Pick a menu for me,* but work with the caterer to choose a menu and overall plan that reflects their own style and vision.

NICE TOUCH

If you've enjoyed working with particular servers on a caterer's staff, ask that they work your next event, too. It's nice to know the names of people working in your home.

Be clear about the services you want the caterer to provide. Will they serve the food as well as prepare it? Will they supply plates, dinnerware and glasses? Will they arrange for other rentals, such as tables and chairs and linens? Will they handle the bartending as well as the food? Will they clean up at the end of the party? Will they take care of the flowers and decorations? Do you want the catering staff to help with any additional tasks, such as answering the door and checking coats?

If you meet the caterer in your home, which is a good idea if that's where you'll be entertaining, show her the kitchen so she is aware of any potential issues. If you plan on using any of your own serving platters, plates or glassware for the event, check with the caterer to make sure that you have the necessary quantities on hand. It's very frustrating for a caterer to show up for a job only to find that critical components of the service are missing.

After your initial meeting, the caterer should put together a sample menu or two with per-person price estimates. Before committing to the caterer also ask for an itemized breakdown of the costs for food, staff and rental equipment. Clarify whether taxes and gratuities are included in your quoted price and what the payment schedule will be. And make sure the contract you eventually sign matches the terms you've agreed to verbally.

Once you have the rough outline of your event in place, you and the caterer should work together to fine-tune the details. But whatever adjustments you make, avoid skimping on the amount of food or the number of staff that is recommended. Caterers are experts at knowing how much food to have on hand and how many people they need to serve it. The staffing needs for a particular event will depend on both the number of guests and the level of formality: Generally, for a large seated dinner you'll need about one-and-a-half staff members for every ten guests. Less formal events require less service. Guests can pour their own wine at the table, for example. A good caterer wants your event to succeed as much as you do, and having adequate staff is a big part of that success.

Confirm all the details a week or so before your event and check in again the day before. When the caterer's team arrives, help get them oriented. Check in with them periodically, but unless something seems amiss to you, try to stay out of their way and let them do the work you're paying them for. This means keeping kids, pets and inquisitive guests out of the kitchen.

.Bartenders

Whether or not you're enlisting the services of a caterer, hiring professional bartending help can be a smart idea, even for a smaller event. For a cocktail party with more than twenty-five guests, hiring a bartender plus a server to pass drinks will prevent traffic jams at the bar. Even if you're having as few as fifteen guests, if you want to offer a full range of cocktails and don't want to tend bar all night, consider hiring one drink server so you are free to handle the more enjoyable host duties.

The cost of professional bartending services varies by region, but you can expect to pay between $15 and $25 an hour plus the tip. Get recommendations from friends, caterers and party planners. Professional bartenders should come prepared with a bar kit that includes a wine opener, pour spouts, a cocktail shaker, a strainer, long-handled spoons, towels and a knife. As the host, you'll be expected to provide the raw materials, including the liquor, mixers, ice, glasses and adequate work space. If you're not sure what types and quantities of liquor and extras you should have on hand, be sure to ask the bartender's advice.

Rentals

When you're throwing a party for a big crowd, using the china, glassware, flatware and linens from a party-rental company is a no-brainer. They're also the place to go for any extra tables and chairs you might need. Aside from the fact that few of us have fifty table settings on hand, renting makes sense from a stress- and labor-saving perspective. If a guest breaks a glass or a plate, you can breathe a sigh of relief that it's not your glass or plate. And when the party's over, you're done, too, as rental companies do the dishwashing and laundry.

Renting supplies can be a smart move for smaller parties as well. You may want to give your usual table setting a facelift with fancy rented china, serving platters and linens. (High-end party-rental companies offer an array of styles.) Consider them for a cocktail party when you desire just the right glass for every drink order and a couple of professional icing tubs for chilling bottles of beer, wine and Champagne. And don't overlook renting basics such as coat-racks, hangers and oversize trash cans. They'll make your event go a little more smoothly.

Most caterers have rental companies they regularly work with, and your caterer will likely want to make the necessary arrangements with them directly. If you're not working with a caterer, call a few in your area to ask which rental companies they work with, then com-pare prices and services. Also, inquire about their minimum order and whether delivery or additional charges apply.

Be sure to take advantage of one of the greatest resources a good rental company has to offer—its staff. A knowledgeable rental-company rep will make sure you have all the supplies you need with the right quantities for the number of people you're having and will suggest any items you have not thought of. (They should also steer you away from anything you really don't need.)

Rental companies typically deliver the day of, or day before an event and pick up the day after. Clarify the preferred method and terms of payment before the scheduled delivery. Payment is usually due when the items are dropped off.

HOSTING A PARTY IN A RESTAURANT OR COUNTRY CLUB

If you have more friends than you have room to entertain them, or you simply prefer the convenience of having someone else do the cooking and cleanup, then hosting a sit-down dinner at a restaurant or country club may be the perfect solution. And it generally costs less than catering a party at home.

Pick a place where the food has broad appeal (sushi or Ethiopian cuisine may be intimidating for some). If you're throwing the party for a guest of honor, keep his or her favorites in mind. It goes without saying, but make sure to actually have a meal—or even several—at the restaurant or club before booking it for your party. In addition to checking out the food, pay attention to the service and the overall setting. Look for a place with a comfortable bar area where guests can mingle for awhile before sitting down to dinner. Indicate the times for cocktails and for dinner on your invitation.

When you meet with the restaurant manager (a large restaurant that frequently has private parties may have a banquet manager) to plan your event, survey the space where your party will be seated and discuss how the tables will be arranged. If there's a private room for parties, verify that it's roomy enough and not so isolated that the ambience of the restaurant isn't conveyed.

Go over the menu with the manager to determine which dishes you'd like to offer your guests. For small groups, select two or three appetizers, a main course and several dessert options for guests to choose from. For large parties, you may want to choose the entire menu in advance. It's common to select one or two wines to serve with dinner and to let guests order cocktails from the bar when you're gathering there before the meal.

If you want to personalize the event with your own flowers, centerpieces, special place cards or gifts for your guests, discuss your plans with the restaurant manager to coordinate things like delivery and setup. Also, make sure that your centerpieces are the right size for the tables and that any flowers or gifts won't get in the way of the servers.

Arrange to pay your bill in advance or in private to avoid having the bill handed to you at the party. Clarify the tipping protocol. The gratuity for servers may be included in your bill, and it is customary to tip the maître d' something extra before the party.

On the big night, arrive a little early to make sure everything looks right, but let the maître d' greet your guests at the door—that's his job. Let everyone else do his job, too. Be sure to communicate all your wishes ahead of time, so when your party's in full swing, you'll be able to mingle instead of micromanaging the restaurant staff.

A note on invitations: When hosting a party at a restaurant, make sure to include not only the name of the place, but also the address and phone number in addition to your own. This way, a guest who's lost knows where to call for directions. In addition, consider including driving instructions for guests who might not be familiar with the area.

Ask the Expert:
SELECTING WINES LIKE A PRO

If you want to expand your wine horizons beyond the more usual sources of California, Burgundy and Bordeaux and become more attuned to quality, Michele Pravda, co-owner of Smith & Vine in Brooklyn, New York, suggests taking a wine course or even a trip to Italy. Ideal for serving with dinner or presenting as a gift, Amarone-style wines from the Valpolicella region are "fruit-forward"—that is, crowd-pleasing—but good enough to impress wine aficionados. Piedmont wines from the Barolo and Barbaresco areas are also interesting choices, with bottles ranging in price from affordable to quite expensive. "They're delicious," says Pravda, "and they're also a great way of starting a collection, because the older bottles are quite enjoyable." A detour to Spain is also worthwhile. "Rioja is very hot now," Pravda goes on to say.

When she needs a lot of wine for a party, Pravda looks to southern France. The Grenache-heavy wines from the southern Rhône Valley "go with lots of things," says Pravda. "They don't need food" to be enjoyed, like some heavier wines. If you see a southern Rhône blend whose label indicates it came from famed wine importer Kermit Lynch, snatch it up. Other regions of southern France also yield fun, festive wines, and those from Provence and the Languedoc are an especially good value.

To shake things up on the after-dinner-drink tray, Pravda suggests the Italian digestif *amaro*. "It's not sweet like other dessert wines," she says. "And I love that it helps you digest. It also makes a nice aperitif with soda." Good sherry is another favorite. "Jimenez sherry is really dark, deep and raisiny." And Pravda loves the baked apple flavor of aged calvados, the French apple brandy. These after-dinner drinks make great gifts, as they are a thoughtful alternative for hosts who know their wines and would appreciate discovering something new.

There's a whole world of wine out there, and people shouldn't let the fear of looking like tourists deter them from exploring new lands. "People worry too much about wine in general. Because, when you think about it, wine is fun. We try not to be pretentious, not to make wine something that's daunting," says Pravda in conclusion.

Ask the Expert:
FLOWER POWER

"If you'd like to duplicate that dazzling arrangement you saw in an elegant restaurant or posh private party, think twice before going it alone," says Stephanie Foster, a floral designer at Church Street Flowers in San Francisco. "The biggest mistake people make is thinking they can do it themselves," she says. What the professionals make look easy is hardly effortless. Aside from the artful arranging, there's the issue of the flowers themselves. Even if you go to the professional's source, the urban flower market, "the florists always have the first pick," says Foster. "When you get to them, the good ones are long gone."

Another mistake do-it-yourselfers make is failing to consider possible flower allergies. "If you have guests who are allergic to flowers, you need to avoid using anything fragrant, things like lilies, hyacinths and narcissus," Foster says.

People also need to keep in mind that great professional arrangements aren't cheap. "People tend to underestimate cost," Foster says. "For an elegant dinner party at home, for example, you should plan to spend $75 or more for a centerpiece that's nice and dense," the same amount on flowers for the living room and something smaller, in the $25 range, for the bathroom." You might want to adorn the entry, too, and the buffet table or sideboard if you're using one. When making multiple arrangements, Foster always ties together colors from room to room, sticking with a theme throughout the house.

For less formal, impromptu affairs, amateurs need not be daunted, though. Just keep it simple. "It's best to go with bunches of one flower: tulips or sunflowers with the stems cut short or hydrangeas. These flowers look best in a short vase that's square or cylinder-shaped." Get a good pair of clippers or pruning shears or a nice sharp Swiss Army knife or paring knife so you can cleanly cut the stems on an angle right before putting them in water. This ensures good water absorption, which keeps flowers perky. Keep them out of the heat, and use some kind of flower food (a mixture of sugar and bleach) to keep the water clear.

PART II

Being a Good Host

MAKING GUESTS FEEL COMFORTABLE

The Greeting

You've planned perfectly. You're showered, pressed and dressed, the hot hors d'oeuvres are heating and the white wine is chilling. At last, the ring of the doorbell says *Showtime!* Of course, the wise host always expects at least one guest to show up a little early, so have yourself and your home ready at least fifteen minutes early. You don't want to embarrass an enthusiastic guest with the greeting, *I'm still getting dressed.* Try to greet each guest at the door, even if you have to break off a conversation with another guest. If your spouse or other designated cohost is free, it's sufficient for only one of you to greet the newcomer. Two hosts need not stay together all evening; indeed, divide and conquer is a far smarter strategy.

Hug, kiss or shake? With good friends, you'll have already established a comfortable greeting, but less intimate acquaintances present

a challenge. Unless you and your guests are all of the same demonstrably affectionate culture, a handshake is generally the most comfortable greeting for all involved. To make sure you get the shake you want and to avoid the awkward half-hearted hugs and kisses you don't, establish your intentions immediately: Extend your right hand as soon as possible and take a subtle step back if necessary. Your body language will relieve your guest of any uncertainty about the expected greeting. Make sure your handshake is accompanied by direct eye contact and a smile for a warm welcome.

Whether you kiss, hug or shake, make sure to get each guest a drink—and quickly (not forgetting to relieve him of a coat, hat or umbrella). Giving guests a drink to hold instantly makes them feel more comfortable and helps set a celebratory mood. For a larger party, hiring a professional bartender will help ensure that everyone gets a drink—and a well-made one—freeing you for more important hosting duties.

Some hosts like to answer the door with a signature cocktail, Champagne or other welcoming drink already in hand (or on a tray) for the entering guest. While this can require some physical dexterity or a helper to pull off, it can be quite a charming gesture, especially on a hot afternoon (think icy lemonade) or wintry night (hot mulled cider).

Making Introductions

Now that you've greeted your guests, hung up their coats and handed them drinks, don't abandon them, at least not until you've introduced them to someone else. If a small group is gathered in one place, it's courteous to introduce each newcomer to the entire gathering. At a larger party where guests are more scattered, you need to introduce

a new guest to just one other person to get the ball rolling. Naturally, if you have more than one other guest close by, you should make an effort to introduce the new arrival to the *right* person; avoid pairing up two socially awkward types if you can help it.

A good host makes introductions that give people a common link, enabling their conversation to flow easily. If you know that one guest just came back from Pebble Beach, make sure to mention that when introducing her to a fellow golfer. Likewise, two avid movie buffs will surely find plenty to talk about. Your friend planning a trip to Buenos Aires will want to hear about the experiences of another who just came back from there. And so on.

Tradition dictates that in social situations one person should always be introduced *to* another and in a particular order. While some etiquette guides make this sound rather complicated, it's not. Here is everything you need to remember:

- A man is always introduced to a woman. What does this mean exactly? That your introduction follows this format: Woman's name + *I'd like you to meet, may I introduce* or simply *this is* + man's name. For example, *Madeline Stone, I'd like you to meet Miles Wetherby.* **Note:** Saying each person's name once is enough. Feel free to avoid the awkward, *Ms. Stone, meet Mr. Wetherby. Mr. Wetherby, Ms. Stone.*
- A younger person is always introduced to an older person. The wording of your introduction follows the same format as above, saying the older person's name first. *Dr. Wells, this is my niece Charlotte Prince.*

- A less prominent person is always introduced *to* the more important person. Prominence these days is typically less obvious than either age or gender; so long as you're not hosting U.S. senators or Nobel laureates, you needn't worry too much about this rule. If entertaining business colleagues, though, let rank on the corporate ladder be your guide. Introduce a new middle manager *to* the CEO.
- When presenting family members, introduce them to other guests as a matter of courtesy, regardless of the relative's age, gender or station in life: *Andrew Stevens, this is my aunt, Dr. Janice Feinstein.*

A note about names: In all but the most informal situations, first-name-only introductions are best avoided. A last name, after all, is an important bit of information that may help your guests find common ground or steer clear of embarrassing faux pas. When deciding the appropriate level of formality for an introduction, think about the names the people you are introducing would naturally use when talking with one another. With adults of more or less equal standing, use first and last names. When a child is introduced to an older person, it should be to a *Mr., Mrs., Ms.* or *Dr. so-and-so.* And it is respectful to use only last names when introducing exceptionally eminent people: high-ranking government, military or religious officials, for example.

Forgetting Names and Faces

A host who never forgets a name is as admirable as she is rare. If you draw a blank in the midst of your introductions, don't despair. You basically have two options:

The sneaky alternative assumes that you do know the name of at least one of the people you need to introduce. In this case, introduce

HOW TO REMEMBER A NAME

There's nothing quite so frustrating—or embarrassing—as drawing a blank on someone's name, especially the name of someone you've invited to your own party. Here are some tips to help tickle your memory:

- First, pay attention to make sure you hear the name in the first place. If you're in a loud room or the person you're speaking with mumbles, ask him to repeat his name. *I'm sorry, I didn't catch that.* Your guest won't mind repeating it.
- Ask about the pronunciation if it's at all tricky. *That's an interesting name. Let me try it to make sure I'm saying it right.*
- Ask a question about the name, such as how it's spelled.
- Repeat the person's name at least three times in conversation, always ending the conversation with the name.
- Associate the name with a prominent feature, physical characteristic or personality trait of the person. You might give the person a nickname (in your head only) to help you remember: tall Thomas, peppy Paula or confident Christine.
- Look for another simple association that might help you remember the name, such as:
  Same name as a friend, celebrity or famous person
  The name is also an occupation (Baker, Gardener, Tailor)
  The name rhymes with something (Kwan sounds like Swan, for example)
  It has an interesting translation (Morgenstern means morning star)

him or her to the person whose name eludes you, saying something like: *Oh, have you met Emily Johnson yet?* With luck, your nameless guest will identify himself or herself and save you any further embarrassment.

Some people, not entirely without reason, consider this tactic to be rather transparent. If you're one of those people, you'll need to take the high albeit humbling road and politely confess your memory lapse: *I'm sorry, but I'm drawing a blank on your name right now.* And if you think you remember someone's name but are less than absolutely certain, better to opt for either method above than to toss out a dimly remembered name and be way off the mark. (See How to Remember a Name, facing page.)

What if you can't remember someone's face? If you're introduced to someone by one of your guests and can't recall whether you've met this person before (your bachelor uncle, with his revolving cast of women friends, does make it tough), hedge your bets with the flexible greeting, *Nice to see you*, instead of, *Nice to meet you.*

Encouraging Conversation

You've greeted your guests and made all the introductions. The invitees are finding one another uniformly brilliant and charming. There is ample food and drink, and you're nowhere close to running out of ice. It's time to set the party on cruise control, sit back with a cool gin and tonic and bask in the glory of it all.

Enjoy your moment, but don't think your work is done. A gracious host is always on the lookout for party dead spots and other social hazards. Is there a wallflower who needs a conversation starter? Are all your guests clustered in two groups at opposite corners of your living room?

One way to keep people mingling is to ensure they keep moving, giving everyone ample opportunity to bump into someone new. One classic trick is to put the food on one side of the room (or apartment or house) and the drinks on the other. At a cocktail party, make sure to provide less than enough seating for everyone. That's right. A drinks party where everyone remains stuck to his or her seat all night isn't much fun, unless perhaps there's a Ouija board involved. For a longer event, such as a dinner party, keep things fresh by forcing people to switch seats. Serve cocktails in one room, dinner in another and coffee somewhere else.

As the host, you should make it your goal to speak—at least briefly—with each of your guests. Small talk isn't everyone's forte, but you can acquit yourself admirably by following just a few simple strategies:

Remember that people love to talk about themselves, so ask questions. *What do you do for a living?* may be humdrum, but it does the trick in a pinch. Asking someone about his hobbies or last vacation may elicit a more interesting and enthusiastic response. And don't be afraid of sounding superficial. That's why it's called small talk. You'll have time to demonstrate your depth later on if you choose to. Is someone wearing an interesting piece of jewelry or spectacular shoes? These items can mean a lot to people. Ask about them as there's sure to be a good story. Think of yourself as a reporter trying to uncover one memorable or unique fact about each person you speak with.

This doesn't mean you can't talk about yourself. If a guest asks a question about you, reward him with more than a *yes* or *no* answer. If asked what you do, don't just give a job title. And if asked, *Have you read any good books lately?*, don't simply say, *yes*—elaborate.

As with other aspects of entertaining, when it comes to small talk, preparation is key. Make studying up on your guests a part of your

CONVERSATION JUMP-STARTERS

A little skill at small talk is a big advantage in any social situation. Movies, books, travel and work are often good subjects to start with. Memorize a few all-purpose openers and put the fear of the awkward silence behind you:

- *What kind of work do you do?* (With the follow-up: *So, what's happening in your business now?*) Know that in certain European countries, questions about how one makes a living are frowned upon.
- *Have you been to that new restaurant/movie theater/fancy grocery store that just opened in town?*
- *Did you see/read this interesting story about _____ in the news?* Steer clear of any story that forces people to take sides politically if you don't know where the other person stands. Think weather, sports and celebrities.
- *We're planning a vacation for later this year. Where was your last great trip?*
- *How are your children?* Most people love talking about their kids. If you're not sure whether someone has kids, though (or whether someone is married), don't inquire. An awkward answer could cause the conversation to grind to a halt.

party groundwork and you'll be several steps ahead in the small-talk game. You don't need to start an official dossier or even do an online search (although that may turn up something interesting). Just take time to review your guest list in advance and mentally note an interesting fact or two about each person. *Is she involved with a certain charity? Do they have children? Has he been anywhere interesting since the last time you spoke?* If you can't think of anything, ask your spouse or a friend who may know the person better.

No matter how effortlessly fascinating the conversation, though, you can't let any one guest monopolize your time. As a host, remember that your mission is to keep moving. Picture a bee in a garden, buzzing from flower to flower. You can be forgiven for brief conversations. Your guests will understand, and as a host you always have a slew of good excuses: *I need to check on the food. That's the doorbell. I believe the kitchen is on fire.*

Guests of Honor

If you're throwing your party in honor of a special guest, make sure to point him out to any arriving guests who may not recognize him and, if possible, make an introduction. At more formal events you may want to create a receiving line to ensure that each guest has an opportunity to meet the honored guest and vice versa. (Just make sure you have enough space so the line doesn't create a bottleneck.)

HOSTING A DINNER PARTY FOR THE BOSS

If your boss has invited you, with or without your spouse, to a social occasion, you should return the invitation in some way. You do not need to reciprocate in kind. That is, if your boss took you to dinner at a four-star restaurant, you needn't do the same. Inviting your boss to an informal dinner at your home or to a casual restaurant is appropriate.

A few general guidelines:

- Send a written invitation; don't phone or use e-mail.
- It might be easier to entertain your boss if you invite other people over, too. Think about people with similar interests to make sure conversation flows.
- If you normally call your boss Mr. or Ms. at the office, don't suddenly shift to first-name familiarity, unless your boss suggests it.
- On the other hand, be yourself. Entertain as you normally do: Don't hire help if you wouldn't normally do so and don't serve expensive or difficult-to-make foods just to impress. For one thing, the boss might get the impression that you don't really need that upcoming raise after all. It's also difficult to be gracious and interested in conversation when you're trying hard to impress.
- Finally, watch the alcohol consumption—both your own and your spouse's. Loose lips can sink not only ships, but careers, too.

HANDLING AWKWARD SITUATIONS

The Unexpected Guest

An element of surprise is a good thing for a party. But you might not feel this way when a guest who didn't respond to an invitation shows up ready to eat and drink, or when someone arrives with an unexpected friend.

Strive to greet a surprise guest as graciously as your expected ones, with a warm smile and a drink. Refrain from saying anything that would make the drop-in or the person who brought him or her uncomfortable. At an opportune moment after the party you might tell the friend that as much as you enjoyed meeting the unexpected guest, you'd appreciate advance notice the next time.

If you're hosting a cocktail party or casual buffet, an extra body or two shouldn't be too hard to accommodate. A sit-down dinner, however, poses more of a challenge. You'll need to squeeze in an extra place setting and marshall your creativity in the kitchen. If you've planned on serving each guest a whole filet mignon, for example, serve sliced filet mignon instead. (Giving up your own main course for the unexpected guest will only create more awkwardness.) Throw some extra lettuce into your salad and whip up some extra pasta, rice or other easy-to-make side dish; no one need go hungry.

The Intoxicated Guest

When a guest has had too much to drink, your most important responsibility is to make sure she gets home safely. Second, try to minimize any embarrassment she may cause herself or the other guests.

If you spot a guest hitting the slippery slope between "quite a lot" and "too much," help her put on the brakes. Take her aside and suggest a cup of coffee or a soft drink instead of another cocktail. Hopefully, she'll get the hint.

Should the situation be more dire, if a guest is sick, stumbling or surly, first seek help from the person or people she came with or another friend. Get your guest safely off her feet in a quiet room or, better yet, on her way home with someone else driving. If there's no one available to provide a ride, call a cab and give the driver directions. Or, have her spend the night.

If an inebriated guest attempts to get behind the wheel, you are permitted—indeed required—to use any means necessary to separate her from her car keys. Not only is there the potential for serious harm to your guest and whomever she might encounter on the road, but as her host you could be found legally liable for any resulting injuries.

The Guest Who Won't Leave

You've done such a good job making guests feel at home that—guess what?—a few of them just don't want to leave. There are a number of ways to deal with guests who can't seem to call it a night.

Remember, prevention is the best medicine. Start giving off time-to-go clues about a half hour before you'd like your last guest to be gone: Give a last call for drinks, bring out the coffee and turn up the lights (ideally, they're on a dimmer so you can do it gradually). At a casual dinner gathering you can start clearing the table. Asking guests to lend a hand is a good way to help would-be loafers find their feet or the door. Don't lose yourself among the dirty dishes in the sink, though. That's not the effortless impression you want to leave your guests with.

No matter how clear your cues, however, there are those guests who just can't take a hint. If the lingerers are close friends who know how to show themselves out or if you have staff to clean and close up for you, you might follow the John and Jackie Kennedy model: say good-night and invite your guests to party on. *Well, we're exhausted, but we wouldn't want to break up such a good time. Who's making breakfast?*

If this isn't an option you're comfortable with, ask someone what time it is. Act surprised when she tells you. *Really! I had no idea.* If that doesn't break things up, you'll just have to be more direct: *It's really getting late, and we need to be up early.*

The Guest Who Breaks Something

Crash! Yes, that's your great aunt's crystal vase in pieces on the floor. And the stammering, red-faced guest who knocked it over is just as horrified as you are. Try to smooth things over with a joke or reassuring word. If that's too much to ask, at least hold back your tears and avoid saying anything to make the vase-breaker feel any worse. If someone breaks a glass or plate at the table, get him a replacement as quickly and discreetly as possible to help minimize his embarrassment.

A well-mannered guest, of course, should offer to replace or repair the item she has damaged or to otherwise make amends. If a guest insists on paying for a broken item, you may politely decline the offer. But if she persists, you may give her an estimate of the cost. If the guest doesn't offer to do anything, no matter how great the loss, it's not your place to push. Just don't invite her back for future events.

Remember that accidents do happen, and it's a rare festive gathering that ends without some innocent object getting broken, stained or otherwise roughed up. Try to minimize the potential damage by putting away anything of great value, either monetary or sentimental, before your guests arrive.

The Argumentative Guest

What about the guest who becomes belligerent or offensive? If too much drink is a factor, see The Intoxicated Guest, on page 63. If it's really a personality or bad-mood problem, ignoring it is usually a better tack.

A guest who makes off-color, sexist, racist or otherwise offensive jokes in your presence doesn't deserve even half-hearted polite laughter. Quickly changing the subject or simply walking away sends a disapproving message without making a scene. If the joke is particularly offensive to someone within earshot, privately apologize for your rude guest to the offended party. If you've heard the joke before or can see pretty well where it's heading, you might try to break off the teller before he can get to the punch line. Ask him for help opening a bottle of wine, or a window *in another room*. With any luck, he'll forget about the joke he has left hanging.

A combative guest calls for a similar distraction tactic. While there is a fine line between animated discussion and argument, some people enjoy a heated debate with their cocktails. If other guests appear uncomfortable with someone's level of intensity, or if the views expressed are offensive, make sure to intervene. Don't take on the person directly, as that may only cause matters to escalate. Just butt in with a subject-changer. Ask someone else a question *(Mia, tell us about your trip to Spain.)*, or divert the arguer with an alternate subject likely to capture his interest. *(Henry, you're the wine expert. What can you tell me about this chardonnay? It was highly recommended by my neighborhood wine merchant.)*

PARTY PROTOCOL

Invitations

The type of event you've decided to host determines the kind of invitation you need to send and when you send it. Less formal affairs require less notice. Last-minute invitations are fine for something informal and spontaneous, but as a rule, sending out invitations as far in advance as possible shows guests that you value their time and their company.

While very formal events still call for the traditional engraved invitation, less formal events, from dinner parties to barbecues, may be properly announced with handwritten or printed invitations sent by mail, phone calls or e-mail. It all depends on the impression you want to give, the expectations you want (or don't want) to raise and the expectations of your intended guests. There are advantages to each method: A mailed invitation, the most formal choice and never incorrect, 'not only signals your guests to expect something special but also provides them with a convenient reminder of the details of your event. A written invitation can take many forms—it doesn't have to be formal or fancy. Your party invitations are a great way to show some humor and creativity, and if you have a computer at home, you have the wherewithal to create them yourself, either from scratch or using templates available online. Invitations by phone are expedient—an instant RSVP!—and entirely appropriate for many occasions, but then e-mail, fax or call again to confirm. E-mail invitations are convenient and efficient if all your intended guests have an e-mail account that they regularly check. Whatever medium you choose, it's a good idea to invite all your guests in the same way. Someone might feel slighted to learn that everyone else at the party received a written invitation, if he received only a phone call.

If you're planning an event that depends on certain key people for its success, call them first to confirm their availability for your intended date, then follow up with written invitations, if you're sending them. For elaborate formal occasions and at busy times of year, such as during the Christmas holidays and the Fourth of July, think about sending save-the-date notices six weeks or more before the event.

Invitation Lead Times

TYPE OF PARTY	SEND INVITATIONS
Cocktail party	Two to three weeks before, or longer during the holiday season
Informal dinner	A few days to three weeks before
Formal dinner	Three to six weeks before
Christmas holiday party	One month before
Anniversary or birthday party	Three to six weeks before
Lunch or tea	A few days to three weeks before
Weekend at your home	Two to three months in advance

No matter what form your invitation takes, it should always deliver the following information:

- **WHO IS HOSTING.**
- **THE KIND OF PARTY.** Be as specific as you can so guests know what to expect and can prepare appropriately. How formal will it be? What will you be offering in terms of food and drink? If it's a cocktail party only, say so; that way guests will know they should make other dinner plans. If it's a dinner party, will you be serving drinks first?
- **THE DATE AND TIME.** Again, be specific: *Drinks at 6:00, dinner at 7:00* or *Cocktails, 5 to 7:30 P.M.*, for example. Supplying an ending time is standard practice for cocktail parties. You might also want to include an ending time if you're hosting a party for children, an event preceding another event (such as cocktails and

hors d'oeuvres before a show) or an open house where guests are invited to stop in anytime within a prescribed start and ending time.

- **THE LOCATION AND ADDRESS.**
- **RSVP INFORMATION.** If you want guests to respond, give them a way to get in touch with you: a phone number, address and, if it suits you, an e-mail address, along with the deadline for doing so, if you wish. If you care about getting an accurate head count, avoid the "Regrets only" wording.
- **INCLUDE ANYTHING ELSE YOUR GUESTS NEED TO KNOW TO FEEL COMFORTABLE AT YOUR PARTY.** Is there a dress requirement? Is it a surprise party? Are gifts expected or discouraged?
- **FINALLY, BE CLEAR ABOUT EXACTLY WHO IS INVITED.** If you're mailing invitations, write the name of each person you are inviting when addressing the envelopes. If you're getting the word out via phone, say *We hope you and John can join us next weekend*, pointedly leaving out the names of their children. If guests are free to bring others, say so in your invitation. *Please bring a guest! The more the merrier!*

If you don't request responses with an RSVP or ask for "Regrets only," you can expect 70 to 80 percent of those you've invited to show up for a cocktail party or buffet. And if you do ask guests to RSVP, add 10 or 20 percent to the number of acceptances you actually receive. If you're concerned about getting an exact head count for a small dinner party, for example, and haven't heard from everyone, by all means pick up the phone and call or e-mail to confirm. It's not pushy to seek a definite reply. It is rude not to respond to an invitation.

Seating Arrangements

Once you've accumulated your RSVPs, when you're hosting a formal dinner, it's time to start thinking about the seating arrangements. Even if you choose to forgo formal place cards, it's nice to have a seating plan in your head so you can direct guests to the seats you've chosen for them. By the way, good guests always sit where you tell them to.

The goal of your seating plan should be to mix things up, to create interesting pairings, and to ensure that people are comfortable. Some general guidelines:

- You and your spouse should sit at opposite ends of the table. If your guests are seated at more than one table, you and your spouse should split up and sit at different tables.
- Separate couples and close friends to make them talk to someone new. You might make an exception for couples who are newlyweds or newly dating and might not feel comfortable being split up.
- Tradition calls for putting men and women in alternating seats. While this is a nice idea if you're hosting several couples, feel free to ignore it if your guest list isn't a fifty-fifty mix.
- Don't cluster the strong conversationalists: spread them around and seat them near good listeners.
- If possible, sit anyone you know is left-handed at the left end of either side of the table where they're less likely to bump elbows with the righties.
- Put together people who haven't met before or who might not otherwise get the chance to meet, so long as you think they'll have something to talk about.
- At the same time, be sensitive to potential clashes. Avoid seating people you know to be on opposite sides of a sensitive issue next to each other.

- Seating a guest or guests of honor follows a particular set of rules: A female guest of honor sits to the right of the host while an honored male guest sits to the right of the hostess. When a single person is hosting a formal dinner, the guest of honor can be seated either next to, or across from, the host or hostess.

Making a Toast

Given the widespread fear of public speaking, it's not surprising that many, if not most, people feel intimidated when it comes time to propose a toast. Confidence comes with practice, though, and it may help to remember that the whole point of a toast is to make people feel good, and that requires fewer and simpler words than you might think. Spend some time in advance of the occasion thinking about what you'd like to say, whether you simply want to welcome your guests with a toast at the start of the evening or are toasting a guest of honor. A good toast is always thought out in advance, and you'll feel more confident and won't be casting about for the right words if you've prepared.

If you're hosting a dinner at your home or at a restaurant, it is traditional to offer a welcome toast to your guests. At a larger affair you should stand up to deliver your toast. It will help get people's attention and project your voice. Unless there's really no other way to quiet a crowded room, avoid getting your guests' attention by tapping on a glass with your spoon. Instead, politely clear your throat and announce, *I'd like to say something.* If you are having just a few guests for a more intimate dinner, you may sit for the toast.

When your guests' wineglasses have been filled, raise your glass and speak clearly. At an intimate gathering try to make eye contact with each of your guests; if you are toasting a guest of honor, keep focused on him or her as you speak. What you say, obviously, depends on the occasion. You don't need to dazzle. *We're so happy to see such good friends here tonight. Welcome, everyone—and enjoy!* is enough to make everyone feel special. A simple toast to health or to life is always appropriate. If you're aware of any good news concerning any of your guests, such as a promotion, an award or a child's acceptance to college, by all means work that into your toast.

When you've finished speaking, and it's always best to err on the side of brevity, take a sip from your glass and be seated. If a guest returns your toast, you needn't raise your glass or even pick it up. Simply smile in acknowledgment and add a polite *thank you* if you wish. Drinking to oneself is not permitted.

Remember that humor can lend a toast real sparkle, but if you're not a natural joke teller, don't feel you must be funny. Kindness and sincerity are enough. If you are comically inclined, don't use your toast as an opportunity to practice your stand-up act. Keep 'em wanting more, as they say, and restrict yourself to a couple of choice *bon mots* that are in good taste, of course.

Canceling an Event

If you need to cancel or reschedule an event for which you've already sent out invitations, contact all the invited guests as soon as possible.

Phone or e-mail those who regularly check their inbox if you must cancel on very short notice, and make an effort to ensure the message has been received. That is, try to get the actual person on the phone rather than just leaving a message on the voicemail (or with their grade-schooler). If you're rescheduling your event for another date, let guests know when you call. Invitations to formal events should should be recalled with a printed card if time allows.

Surprise Parties

No matter what the occasion, whether a birthday, an anniversary or a new job, the most important thing to consider before planning a surprise party is whether the person you're planning it for would enjoy such a surprise. Being the guest of honor at a surprise party, believe it or not, is some people's worst nightmare. And having to feign surprise because the cat somehow got out of the bag only makes it worse. So plan carefully, making sure all the invited guests understand that it's a surprise party and figure out a fail-safe way of delivering the honoree without raising his or her suspicions.

It helps to enlist an assistant, such as the spouse or a close friend of the honoree, to create a fake activity for him to attend. Let any guests who may have contact with the honoree know about the planned strategy for tricking the guest of honor and help them come up with a fictitious plan for the party date if they're asked. If you know someone is not good at keeping secrets, encourage him to avoid the honoree until party time. Invite all the guests to arrive at least thirty minutes before the guest of honor, and if people are driving to the party, ask them to park out of sight if the presence of familiar cars would be an obvious giveaway.

Pets

Dogs, especially big ones, can be overwhelming at an indoor party. Allergic or pet-phobic guests may be made especially uncomfortable. While cats usually hide in a quiet corner when there's lots of company, for the comfort of all your guests consider putting pets outside or in a closed-off part of your home before company arrives.

Children

If you don't want children at your party, there's no need to say so in your invitation. (*No Kids!* is a bit unfriendly.) Instead, if you have any concern that your invitees may not understand that your cocktail party is for adults only, subtly express your wishes when guests call to RSVP: *I hope you won't have any trouble finding a sitter for Saturday night.*

AT THE TABLE

Serving Food

The formality of the occasion dictates the "proper" manner of serving food. A formal dinner is defined by an elaborate set of rules and traditions, while the customs for less formal occasions stress convenience and common courtesy. Keep in mind that entertaining today, especially when you're hosting people at home, is far more relaxed, informal and less reliant on the strict rules of etiquette that once held sway. For the most part those staid dinner parties of Edith Wharton's day are a thing of the past. They do still occur, but rarely, and only in the most exalted of circumstances. The following are some basic guide-

lines for formal, informal and buffet food service. Adapt them to your own style of entertaining as grand or graciously simple as that may be.

Formal Meals

At the most formal kind of dinner, guests never serve themselves: they are served by professional staff. Serving platters are never placed on the table, the meat is carved in the kitchen and the vegetables, bread and condiments are passed and placed on a side table or returned to the kitchen. Here are some other elements of formal dinner service:

- The dinner consists of four or more courses.
- The main course is often presented to the hostess for inspection before serving.
- Because the formal dinner consists of multiple courses, second helpings are not offered.
- Hot food is served on a warm plate; plates for salad and other cold items are cool to the touch.
- The place in front of each guest is never left empty. When the meal starts, each place is set with a large (12-inch) service plate, also called a charger. The first-course plate is put on top of the

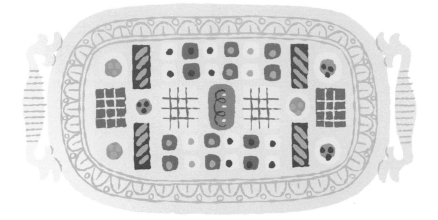

service plate, and when the first course is cleared, the service plate remains on the table until it is exchanged for the hot plate holding the entrée. Subsequent courses, such as the salad, which in formal service comes after the entrée, always involve a simultaneous exchange of one plate for the next. When everyone has finished eating the final savory course, all the plates are removed and the table is made ready for dessert. Dessert plates are then set right on the tablecloth.

- Before dessert is served, a server or butler stands to the left of each guest and crumbs his or her place with a brush or folded napkin.
- Food service proceeds counterclockwise around the table, starting with the guest of honor seated to the right of the host or hostess. Drink service proceeds clockwise to the left. The host is served last. If there is enough help for a large dinner, all the ladies may be served first, starting with the female guest of honor.
- Plates are served and cleared from the left side, while beverages are served and cleared from the right. Except for the first course and the dessert, when two plates may be brought to the table, plates are served and cleared one at a time.

Informal Meals

If all the foregoing sounds a bit nerve-wracking, the truth is, it can be. That's why this kind of very formal meal is usually enjoyed at homes where there is a domestic staff to serve, clear and cook. But informal meals have their rules, too, which you're free to interpret as strictly as you see fit.

- Up to three or four courses are served. The host or hostess should plan the meal so that he or she needs to get up from the table no more than two or three times. It's generally more comfortable for guests if the host or hostess remains at the table. This way they don't feel abandoned.
- Try to have the first course, especially if it's cold, already at each place when guests sit down. Water glasses, which are optional unless you're serving a very spicy meal, should already be filled.
- Food may be served directly from the kitchen, from the head of the table by the host or hostess or on serving plates that are passed family style. In all cases, service proceeds counterclock-wise, starting with the person at the host's right with the host served last.
- When passing dinner plates from the head of the table, each guest takes the plate from the person on his left and passes it to the right until the plate reaches the person at the end of the table. (If there is a woman seated to the host's right, she keeps the first plate, then the second plate is passed to the end of the table.) The next plate is passed to the farthest person on the right side and so on, until everyone to the host's right has been served. The host then passes plates in the same manner to the people seated to his left, serving himself last. If the hostess is serving, the same order is followed from her end of the table, with the guests to her right served first.

- In family-style dining, the host or hostess serves the main dish, such as a roast, as above, then passes the bowls or platters containing the side dishes counterclockwise with guests serving themselves.
- If you are passing serving platters, each dish is passed along with the necessary serving utensils.
- When plates are brought directly from the kitchen, food is served from the left and plates are cleared from the right. **Tip:** *remove* and *right* both begin with the letter *r.*
- To avoid having their food get cold while waiting for others to be served, encourage guests to begin eating as soon as three or four people have been served.
- Bread and other condiments are usually passed by the guests themselves.
- Unlike formal dinners, seconds are usually offered and encouraged. If any food remains after the first service, place the serving platters on a side table or keep them warm in the kitchen and pass them around again when you see that guests are ready for another portion.
- Coffee may be served at the table or in another room. After-dinner drinks are entirely optional.
- A smart division of labor makes the meal appear effortless. At dinners with both a host and hostess, the host traditionally pours the predinner cocktails, passes the hors d'oeuvres, pours the wine at the meal, carves the meat, offers after-dinner drinks and helps guests with their coats. The hostess cooks, sets the table, serves the meal, clears the table and pours after-dinner coffee. Feel free to adjust these job assignments, but discuss who will do what beforehand.

Buffet Service

Almost everything for a buffet is done in advance, so you have plenty of time to spend with your guests. Here are a few tips for making your buffet run as smoothly as possible:

- If the party is large and the room is big enough, put the buffet table in the center of the room and divide each dish of food between two platters, one on each side of the table, so that two lines of people can serve themselves at the same time. Place a stack of plates at the start of each line. To allow for second servings, put out 25 percent more plates than you have guests.

- Lay flatware at the end of the table, with the napkins placed so they're the last thing guests have to pick up. Or wrap a set of utensils in each napkin and place them in a basket for guests to easily take.

- If you like, write the names of the dishes on small cards. At a large buffet this will help keep traffic moving as no one will have to inspect each dish closely to figure out what it is.

- On the buffet table leave enough room so guests can rest their plates beside any dishes that require two hands to serve, such as the salad.

- Place the drinks and glasses on a separate table or sideboard, if possible. Don't forget to provide coasters or cocktail napkins. If possible, serve coffee and dessert at a separate side table.

- If you don't have a large buffet table (at least 5 feet long), use three or four smaller tables instead: one for the tableware, one for the food, one for dessert and dessert plates and a fourth for the beverages.

- For a seated buffet, place the silverware, napkins, wineglasses and water glasses at your guests' places, whether it's a dinner table or several smaller tables. Fill the water glasses before guests sit down, but serve the wine once guests are seated or put an opened bottle on each table.

- When all your guests have arrived and had cocktails, if you've allotted time for that, invite them to serve themselves. At a large party stagger the invitation time to avoid a bottleneck at the buffet table.
- Clear side tables so guests have someplace to put their dirty dishes.

Serving Wine

If you've ever watched a restaurant sommelier at work, you know that the proper service of wine is an art. But the basics of wine service can—and should—be mastered by every gracious host.

Good wine stewardship begins before the bottle is opened. The serving temperature is very important. Remember that once it's out of the bottle and in the glass, wine can be warmed up but not cooled down, so it's better to err on the cold side. Keep in mind that red wine is often served too warm and white wine is often served too cold. Chill white wine to around 45°F. (Allow two hours in the refrigerator or in an ice bucket filled half with ice and half with water. If the entire bottle isn't poured at once, return it to the bucket or a wine-bottle thermos to keep it chilled. Red wine should be served at cellar temperature, which means somewhere around 65°F. If your house is warm, refrigerate the reds ahead of time and take them out shortly before your guests arrive so the wines have time to warm up to the right temperature. Depending on the age and/or quality of the wine, consider decanting it (see How to Decant a Bottle of Wine on page

128). White wines don't need to breathe and can be enjoyed immediately after uncorking.

When you're entertaining at home, have wines uncorked and ready to serve before your guests sit down. If you're serving more than one wine with the meal, the general rule is to move from white to red, dry to sweet, sparkling to still. Your table should be set with a glass for each wine you plan to serve, lined up from right to left in the order they will be used, with the water goblet on the far left. Wineglasses may also be clustered in a triangle, with the white wineglass at the top, the red wineglass at the bottom right and the water glass at the bottom left. The intended order of use is clear and the larger glasses don't camouflage smaller ones. Glasses should remain on the table throughout the meal so that guests can continue to enjoy the wine.

Uncork at least one or two bottles before your guests sit down. When you do so, make sure to cut away all of the foil from the top. If you don't, the wine may pick up an unpleasant metallic taste as it is poured. Use a clean damp cloth to wipe the outside and inside of the lip of the bottle to remove any traces of cork. If you see any bits of cork floating at the top of the bottle, pour a bit of the wine into the sink to remove it. And when you open the wine, don't forget to have a taste from each bottle to make sure none has an "off" taste— you don't want to discover the wine is bad after you've poured a glass for each of your guests.

As the host of a small dinner party, you might want to stand up and pour the first glass for each of your guests, starting with the person to your right and proceeding counterclockwise, filling your own glass last. While pouring, make use of one of the sommelier's favorite tools—a cloth napkin (or *serviette,* in wine-speak, a.k.a. French). Hold it beneath the neck of the bottle as you're pouring to catch any drips, and wipe it around the outside of the neck of the bottle to clean up as you go. When you're pouring white wine, lightly wrap the napkin around the neck to keep the bottle from losing its chill. Always bring the bottle to the wineglass, and pour the wine down the inside of the glass, not straight into the bottom, gently twisting the bottle as you finish pouring to reduce drips.

Wineglasses should be filled no more than about halfway. You want to leave enough space to allow guests to gently swirl the wine to release its bouquet. Because sparkling wines aren't swirled, Champagne flutes should be filled three-quarters full. To help preserve the bubbles, pour sparkling wine down along the sides of the flute.

Once you've served the first glass, place an open bottle at each end of the table, the white at one end and the red at the other if you're serving both, and invite guests to refill their own glasses or ask someone at each end of the table to help keep the wine flowing. If you're having a seated dinner for eight or more, place bottles of red wine and white wine at each end of the table.

Clearing the Table and Cleaning Up

At a large dinner, you or your help can start clearing plates when the majority of guests have finished eating; at a small party, it's most polite to wait until the slowest eater has finished eating before removing anyone's plate.

Serving dishes and platters are removed first, then the plates. Plates are *never* stacked. Take one in each hand and make as many trips as necessary or use a serving tray if you want to carry more. Flatware and stemware are removed third, and small items, such as salt and pepper shakers, are removed last (a tray makes removing these small items easier).

There is no need to clear the dessert plates when dinner is over, unless you plan to move to a nearby sitting area where the sight (or smell) of the dirty dishes might be an unpleasant distraction. In that case, quickly remove them to the kitchen and return to your guests.

Washing dishes, as a rule, should always wait until your guests have departed, unless the party is catered. You can make an exception at a very informal gathering if a friend or two offers to help out. Just make sure your spouse or cohost remains to entertain the rest of your company and don't disappear for too long.

Ask the Expert:

PARTY-RENTAL CLEANUP SECRETS

The largest party-rental company in the Northeast, Party Rental Ltd., handles 30,000 pieces of flatware in an average week. So it's safe to say they know something about cleaning it, as well as glasses and table linens. While some of their methods require special equipment, many of their tricks can be adapted for party cleanup at home.

All Party Rental's flatware is stainless steel or silver- or gold-plated. They don't rent or clean silver. When flatware comes back to them, "It's free from food, but dirty, and there's lots of grease. We sort the flatware—forks, knives and spoons—into separate bins," says Rawle Jonas, general manager of operations. It then goes into an aluminum foil–lined container that is filled with water and an industrial degreasing product (Soilmaster). The grease rises to the top, and any tarnish from the silverware adheres to the aluminum foil, turning it brown. After degreasing, the flatware takes a tumble in a special burnishing machine that cleans and polishes it. It's then rinsed in hot water, hand-dried with a cotton cloth and put away in plastic bags until it's called for again.

Don't feel bad about letting those dirty wineglasses wait till tomorrow; the pros do. "Glasses are washed to order," says Jonas. When they come back dirty, his team simply turns them upside down to let any liquid residue drain out. When they've dripped dry, the glasses are put into racks and stacked up till they're needed again, at which time they're put through the washing machine with specially purified water, detergent and a rinse additive in the final wash. Glasses are kept presentable and dust-free on their way to the next party with a layer of plastic wrap.

When it comes to dishes, the rule is to scrape and soak. To avoid clogged drains and broken-down dishwashers, "Scrape as much as you can into the garbage. Use a knife or spatula, but nothing too abrasive; no Brillo pads on plates," says Jonas. And if there's a lot of food residue remaining on the plates, or you can't wash them right away, Jonas suggests letting them soak in soapy water to keep the grease from hardening.

At Party Rental, tablecloths are checked for stains and burns as soon as they come back. Stains are squirted with liquid stain remover and allowed to sit for a few minutes before going into the washing machine. Wax and red wine are the worst things that can befall a tablecloth, and sometimes these stains are just hopeless. If the cloth can't be saved, it's cut down and made into a smaller cloth or napkins.

❧

PART III

Entertaining Overnight Guests

BEFORE YOUR GUESTS ARRIVE

Once you've made the decision to invite guests for an overnight stay, you'll need to begin planning. Sleeping arrangements, menus and activities all need to be planned, not to mention preparing your home.

If you send an invitation weeks or even months in advance, check in with your guests, by phone or by e-mail, a week or so before their visit to confirm all the details. As much as possible, let guests know what to expect. Has the weather been unusually cold, hot, snowy or wet? Have you planned any activities that require special clothes or equipment? Is there anything guests need to know about your schedule, such as previously planned appointments during any part of their visit? If you have pets, it's a good idea to let guests know when they RSVP, as someone who is severely allergic may choose not to visit.

Make sure everyone fully understands the arrival and departure times. Being clear about this ahead of time helps prevent any awkward moments later on. Take the time to give good driving directions, too. If your place is hard to find, mail or e-mail detailed directions so that your guests can print them out and take them along. (Check out Web sites such as maps.google.com or mapquest.com for computer-generated maps and directions.) Inform guests traveling by plane or train of their options for getting to your place and the approximate cost. Decide before you call whether you or your spouse are willing to drive to the airport to pick them up or to send a car service.

The Welcome

If you've been looking forward to a visit from friends you don't often see, you'll probably want to ply them for news and gossip the second they're in the door. Resist the temptation at least long enough to show them their room (or sleeping area) and the bathroom they'll be using. Let them wash up, unpack and change. Treat anyone who hasn't been in your home before to a brief tour, acquainting him with the general layout and the locations of things like phones, lights and temperature controls. Explain how the locks work and supply your guests with an extra set of keys, if necessary. Show them where to find food and drink they can help themselves to, and be sure to point out anything that's off-limits, like those peaches you're saving for a pie. It's also a good idea to go over the typical daily routine at your house; that the kids are usually up and about by 7 A.M., or that your husband isn't usually back in time for dinner on weekdays.

Accommodations

A gracious and comfortable guest room need not be a room at all. If you don't have a spare bedroom, a pullout sofa, air mattress, futon or feather bed in the den or living room will do. Just make sure guests are aware of the accommodations you're able to offer ahead of time. Some people may choose not to stay over if they don't have a room to call their own. Don't take it personally and don't feel like you have to give up your own bedroom for guests. Your generosity would surely make them feel as if they were imposing.

Even if you don't have a real guest room, with a little creative improvisation you can gather enough essentials to make your guest comfortable. Clear off a side table and position it to serve as a nightstand and leave some hangers on a hook on the back of a door if you don't have closet space. (See Bedroom Essentials on page 133.)

If you have ample room and several visitors, figure out ahead of time who will sleep where. Traditionally—and sensibly—the best room or bed goes to the oldest guest or to anyone with a physical condition that calls for extra pampering. Put families with young children as far from other guests as possible. Chances are they'll be up before others. For a short visit, kids can make do with sleeping bags on the floor if beds are at a premium.

If it's unclear whether an unmarried couple wants to share a room, ask the person you are closest with what arrangement he or she prefers. If letting them sleep together makes you uncomfortable, don't hesitate to put them in separate rooms. Just let them know your intentions beforehand.

Children

If children are coming to visit, be sure to childproof your home. Put away anything fragile or extremely valuable, and if the children are very young, cover all the electrical outlets. Many parents travel with their own portable baby cribs, high chairs and strollers, but others may not be able to. Ask friends with children if you can borrow equipment they might not be using, or consider renting it.

FOOD AND BEVERAGES

When it comes to food for houseguests, being hospitable doesn't require running yourself ragged making meals around the clock. After all, few hosts are up to the duties of innkeeper and full-service chef. A great way to do this is to follow the bed and breakfast model and prepare your guests' first meal of the day, letting them fend for themselves at other mealtimes. You may be out at lunchtime anyway, and you might want to enjoy dinner at a restaurant. When you wake up, just put out some pastries from a neighborhood bakery, fresh fruit and cold cereal with milk, juice and a pot of coffee kept warm in a thermos pitcher. Your guests can then breakfast at their leisure, and you don't have to worry about the eggs or pancakes getting cold.

If you're in a remote location in the country, however, eating at the house may be your only real option. In this case, you've got some planning to do. When you call your guests to confirm the details of their visit, ask about any dietary restrictions and map out your menus accordingly. Stock the kitchen and pantry in advance to cut down on prep time when guests are around and cook as much as you can in advance. Think about dishes you can reheat or serve at room temperature, such as lasagna, quiche or roast chicken. And consider buying packaged, pre-washed greens, which are widely available and make it easy to assemble a quick salad.

Another approach that works with a group of friends who all enjoy cooking is to plan the menu together in advance; e-mail is great for this. Then do your shopping together on arrival with each person, couple or family taking a turn showing off at the stove.

ACTIVITIES

In advance of your guests' arrival, give some thought to activities they might enjoy, especially if an activity will require advance reservations. Once they arrive, sit down with your guests again to discuss any activity ideas. Figure out what you'd all like to do together as well as things guests may want to pursue independently. So you don't feel obligated to entertain your guests constantly, and so they don't feel overly dependent on you, provide them with as much useful information as possible. Keep a guest folder filled with maps, public transportation schedules and brochures for local attractions ready for visitors. Buy any local newspapers or magazines that have entertainment and event listings, which will give your guests a chance to decide for themselves what most interests them. If you

NICE TOUCH
If you're entertaining overnight guests, be sure to turn on a hall light and their bedside light before it gets dark so guests don't have to grope their way through unfamiliar space.

ACTIVITIES FOR WEEKEND GUESTS

While overnight guests generally don't expect or want their host to serve as their full-time tour guide, planning some activities for visitors can go a long way toward creating a more fun-filled and memorable stay for all. It's safe to assume that visitors to your beach house have an interest in relaxing and sunbathing, while ski-house guests probably have a love of the slopes. But if you come up short for an idea or just want to mix things up a little, consider these:

- Devote a day or part of a day to a local sporting activity, like hiking, boating or snowshoeing. Do some advance research to find out about locations, the availability of rental equipment and the cost.
- Plan a cultural outing, such as a visit to a local museum or historical society, or sign up for an organized tour focusing on the history, architecture, wildlife or landscape of the area.
- If you have an active visit planned, a long weekend of skiing, for example, you might want to break it up with something more relaxing. Scout out a few places to go antiquing, or schedule massages or facials at a local spa.
- For more ideas, check with the chamber of commerce in your area, peruse a local guidebook or visit a Web site such as www.citysearch.com. You may be surprised at the diversity of activities offered in your hometown.

GREAT GAMES FOR
A RAINY DAY

If bad weather ruins your plans for the day, or if you and your guests simply want to spend a cozy evening at home, organize a game or two. Almost everyone is familiar with these classic games. In the case of charades, no equipment is necessary, just your imagination!

Backgammon

Dominoes

Chess

Checkers

Poker

Scrabble

Monopoly

Trivial Pursuit

Pictionary

Charades

have membership to a museum, zoo or botanic garden, you could lend guests your membership card for free entry. (For additional ideas about activity planning, see page 93.)

If you are invited somewhere while you have houseguests, you shouldn't necessarily expect that your guests are invited, too, as it really depends on the type of event. If the invitation is to a cocktail party or open house, feel free to ask the host if you may bring along a couple of guests. But for a dinner party where the planning is more involved, additional guests may put too much of a burden on the host. In this case, *We'd love to come, but my cousin and her husband are in town visiting* is the best response. This leaves it to the person extending the invitation to suggest that you bring your cousins along. If an invitation does not include your houseguest, it's usually best to turn it down, unless your houseguest is a close friend or relative who's in town for an extended stay and won't mind your absence for a night.

SAYING GOOD-BYE

The night before your guests depart, let them know what to do with their used linens and towels. Discuss any transportation arrangements that need to be made. Do they need to reserve a car to take them to the airport?

When it's time to go, help guests with their bags and do a quick check to make sure they haven't left anything behind. Remember not to bid farewell too hastily after telling them how wonderful it was to have them visit. Reinforce the notion by waiting on the porch, waving good-bye until they're out of sight.

Ask the Expert:

THE FOUR-STAR GUEST EXPERIENCE

"Our predominant philosophy at the Four Seasons is very simple," says Hans Willimann, general manager of the Four Seasons Hotel in Chicago. "Treat others the same way you want to be treated." Obviously, hotels are in the hospitality business; the rest of us are just amateurs with facilities likely to be more limited. But many of the gracious touches that await a Four Seasons guest can be adapted for overnight guests in your home.

The beds in Willimann's hotel are outfitted with a duvet whose cover is refreshed daily. Each bed has four down pillows with two spares in the closet, just in case. (If the staff knows that a returning guest has allergies, there will be no down-filled pillows in the room.) In addition to ample closet space and sturdy hangers, a luggage bench is provided. Lighting is carefully designed so that if one guest wants to read in bed, the person next to her won't be disturbed. Local magazines are always provided for reading, as are a selection of other titles of interest to the Four Seasons' elite guests.

To make your overnight visitor feel as though they're receiving the four-star treatment, Willimann suggests providing bottled water and a clean glass on the bedside table, a few apples or other seasonal fruit, potpourri sachets in the clothes closet and between the guest towels you've left folded on the bed, a guest room TV, Internet access, a coffeepot and air freshener and a clean glass in the bathroom.

To create a personalized welcome for guests, Willimann will sometimes conduct an Internet search to find out more about their interests or accomplishments and, if possible, find a picture of them. "Then when the beds are turned down, we put a bottle of water with their faces on it next to the bed," says Willimann. A visiting musician may find a gift of musical instruments sculpted in chocolate. When it comes to personalization, you have an advantage over the professionals, as you are already familiar with your guests. "Put a picture of your guest in a frame on the bedside table," suggests Willimann. Or stock the room with books or decorations that relate to her interests or hobbies or your shared history.

PART IV

Being a Good Guest

THE PARTY PRESCRIPTION

When you accept an invitation, you enter into a social contract. In exchange for your host's hospitality, you are agreeing to be polite, enthusiastic and respectful. (Being incredibly witty, an accomplished musician and a great dancer are also nice, though not necessary.) Here are a few simple rules to keep you in any host's good graces and on future guest lists, too.

- **IF AN INVITATION CALLS FOR A REPLY, RESPOND PROMPTLY, WITHIN A FEW DAYS IF IT IS A WRITTEN INVITATION.** If an invitation comes by phone, it is perfectly fine to say that you need to check your schedule. But be sure to call back within a day or so. If you can't accept an invitation, there is no need to explain why.

- **DON'T ACCEPT AN INVITATION IF YOU DON'T HONESTLY EXPECT TO ATTEND THE EVENT.** Saying yes, only to back out when a better offer comes along is an unfortunate practice. There are only a few acceptable excuses for canceling on your host: illness, a death in the family or an unavoidable work conflict. If you're facing one of these situations, let your host know as soon as possible.

- **NEVER BRING—OR ASK TO BRING—UNINVITED GUESTS.** If entertaining out-of-town guests prevents you from accepting an invitation, mention this to your host, which gives him the opportunity to extend an invitation to them, too, if he chooses to. Don't ask to bring your children to a party unless the invitation clearly states that kids are welcome.

- **MAKE YOUR HOST AWARE OF ANY DIETARY RESTRIC-
  TIONS WHEN ACCEPTING A DINNER INVITATION,
  ESPECIALLY IF YOU HAVE SEVERE FOOD ALLERGIES.**
  If your dietary restrictions are very exacting or unusual, offer to
  bring a dish that you can eat.
- **ARRIVE ON TIME.** For a dinner invitation, fifteen minutes is
  fashionably late, but if you show up more than a half hour past the
  invitation time, be sure to have a good excuse—and call ahead.
  You have more leeway with cocktail parties, but you should never
  show up less than a half hour before the party's stated end time.
  At all costs, avoid showing up early for any kind of party. If you
  made good time driving, fix your makeup in the car or take a walk
  around the block to kill time rather than surprise your host.
- **RESPECT YOUR HOST'S PROPERTY.** Wipe your feet on the
  doormat, put your drink on a coaster or napkin and don't fiddle
  with furniture or appliances without permission.
- **SIT WHERE YOU'RE SEATED.** Your host put a lot of thought
  into the seating plan. Don't switch place cards or ask to be seated
  elsewhere.
- **DON'T SMOKE INSIDE UNLESS YOUR HOST IS SMOK-
  ING AND INVITES YOU TO DO THE SAME.** If you must
  have a cigarette in a nonsmoking home, ask your host if you may
  step outside. Be sure not to leave cigarette butts lying around in
  your wake.
- **BE SOCIABLE.** That's why you were invited, after all. Make
  polite conversation with other guests, greet newcomers to the
  party and do not monopolize either your hosts or their guest of
  honor. At the dinner table, pay attention to the people sitting
  both to your left and to your right.

- **KNOW WHEN TO LEAVE.** Dinner guests should stay at least an hour after dinner; leaving sooner is rude. On other occasions, let common sense be your guide. At a small gathering, wait till it looks as if everyone else is ready to leave, so you don't inadvertently start a rush for the door. On the other hand, if it's getting late, your host seems tired and no one else seems to be budging, feel free to get up and say good night. Hopefully, the other guests will follow your lead.
- **THANK YOUR HOST.** When you RSVP, thank your host for the invitation. Before you leave a party, find your host and thank her for a lovely evening. Follow up the next day with a phone call to let her know how much you enjoyed the party. For a more formal affair, such as a sit-down dinner, send a handwritten note expressing your thanks within three days of the party. (See Thank-You Notes, page 111.)
- **RETURN YOUR HOST'S HOSPITALITY.** If someone invites you to a private event in his home or an outside venue, some form of reciprocation is required. This doesn't mean that exact repayment is expected. An invitation to a casual dinner at your home is perfectly appropriate reciprocation for an invitation to a lavish cocktail party at a club. But try to extend your invitation within a couple of months of enjoying someone's hospitality.

When You're an Overnight Guest

The greater intimacy and hosting time required when you are an overnight guest calls for greater attention to the rules of etiquette. Many of these, as you will see, are common sense.

DAMAGE CONTROL: WHAT TO DO IF YOU BREAK SOMETHING

If you break, stain, rip, burn or otherwise damage something while you're a guest in someone's home, let your host know right away and offer a sincere apology. Even if it's something small that your host may not notice, it's better to acknowledge the fact than to be found out later.

In addition to apologizing, you must offer to make amends. If something can be cleaned or repaired, offer to pick up the bill. If something is broken beyond repair, be careful what you say. Don't offer to replace something that can't be replaced, whether it's a one-of-a-kind item, or because replacing it would be beyond your budget. Ask your host, *What can I do?* If your host refuses to put you on the hook, make sure to send a note the next day along with a gift whose value reflects the magnitude of the damage done.

- **COME PREPARED.** Bring your own toiletries. Don't expect to use your host's toothpaste, floss, etc.

- **DON'T EVEN ASK ABOUT BRINGING PETS, UNLESS YOU KNOW YOUR HOSTS VERY WELL.** As with kids at dinner parties, assume pets are not invited. And even if someone invites you to bring along your dog to her country house, don't unless he's well behaved, good around children (if your hosts have kids) and respectful of carpets, furniture, yards, etc.

- **IF YOU'RE VISITING WITH KIDS WHO ARE USED TO SNACKING THROUGHOUT THE DAY, COME PREPARED WITH THE NECESSARY TREATS.** Don't expect your hosts—especially if they don't have children—to be stocked up on juice boxes, animal crackers and chocolate kisses. It is your responsibility to make sure your kids follow the house rules regarding where eating is allowed in the home.

- **HELP OUT.** There is perhaps nothing worse than an overnight guest who creates additional housework but doesn't lift a finger to help out. If you use a cup or plate, rinse it and put it in the dishwasher. Strive to make yourself useful whenever you spy an opportunity. And when offering help, be specific. *Let me peel those apples/help you carry those groceries/clear these dishes*, is better than, *Let me know if there's anything I can do*. If, however, your host replies with a firm *no*, don't insist.

- **BE A GOOD SPORT.** If an outing to the beach is planned and you hate sun and sand, cheerfully follow the program for a day. If, on the other hand, your hosts have nothing planned, don't complain. Enjoy the chance to relax or do some exploring on your own. Never sulk or complain.

- **BE NEAT.** Don't leave personal belongings scattered around the house. Keep the guest room and the bathroom tidy. Make your bed each day and clean the sink and bathtub drain when you're done washing up, especially if you're sharing a bathroom with your hosts. Don't leave a wet bath mat crumpled up on the floor, use only those towels and washcloths designated to you and return the toilet seat to the down position.

- **BE GENEROUS.** Treat your hosts to dinner if you're staying more than a few days, and tell them beforehand so they can plan ahead. And pick up the tab for any incidental expenses when you're out together.

- **BE PHONE CONSCIOUS.** Ask permission before using your host's phone or giving out their number so you can be called. If you're calling long-distance, charge the calls to your calling card or home number. But probably the easiest thing to do is to use your cell phone for all your incoming and outgoing calls. To avoid disturbing your hosts, however, turn off the ringer when it's not needed and excuse yourself to another room to make and receive any calls of a minute or more. Also, don't answer your host's phone unless you're asked to do so.

- **GIVE YOUR HOST SOME DOWNTIME.** Think of an activity you can do by yourself for a couple of hours like taking a jog, visiting a museum or doing some shopping to let your host rest up and tend to any personal business that requires attention. Discuss the timing of your solo excursion

with your host so he can make productive (or blissfully unproductive) use of the time off. If your host needs to discuss personal matters while you're around, discreetly excuse yourself.

- **DON'T HOG PRECIOUS RESOURCES.** If hot water is at a premium (many vacation houses have small hot-water heaters), take short showers. Don't settle in for a leisurely bath when everyone is home and there is only one bathroom.
- **DISCUSS ANY OUTSIDE PLANS WITH YOUR HOST.** If you'd like to spend time with other friends in the area, tell your host in advance and ask about the best time to do so. Don't accept any invitations—for yourself or your host—without consulting him first.
- **FOLLOW YOUR HOST'S SCHEDULE AS MUCH AS POSSIBLE.** It's customary for a host to decide when the day is over. Don't turn in for the night before he does. If you stay up late, do so quietly; opt for reading in bed over high-volume TV watching.
- **GO THE EXTRA MILE.** There are things you can safely do without being asked, such as taking the dog out for his morning walk, buying a bag of hot bagels for breakfast or picking up a gallon of milk or a carton of eggs when you see that your host is running low.
- **PLAN YOUR ARRIVAL AND DEPARTURE THOUGHTFULLY.** Let your host know your travel details, including when and how you'll be arriving, and be sure to make and confirm any reservations in advance. You don't want to impose on your host for an extra night because you couldn't get a seat on the plane or train you had hoped to catch.
- **ASK YOUR HOST WHAT TO DO WITH YOUR USED LINENS AND TOWELS.** You can't go wrong by removing the used sheets and loosely folding them at the base of the bed before

you leave, but some hosts, especially those with housekeeping help, may not want you to bother.

- **LEAVE NO TRACE.** Look around and make sure you have all your belongings. Don't expect your host to pack up and ship the sunglasses or pair of sandals you left behind.
- **SEND A THANK-YOU NOTE.** Overnight stays require a hand-written note sent within a couple of days of your return home. (See Thank-You Notes, page 113.)

GIFTS FOR THE HOST

It is not necessary to bring a gift when you are invited to a cocktail party or open house. If you've been invited for dinner, a small gift is customary, though not strictly required.

The most important rule when it comes to gifts is this: Never give your host something extra to worry about. For this reason, gracious guests don't show up at a dinner

NICE TOUCH

While your host for the weekend may adore the silver platter you've given her, one that's just a bit smaller might better fit her cabinets or side table. Enclose a gift receipt and shop at a store that has locations convenient for your host to make an exchange if need be.

party with flowers, which an already harried host must then find a suitable vase for. If you want to give flowers, send them the day before or the morning of the party with a note saying something like, *Looking forward to a wonderful evening!* This is an especially nice gesture if you are the guest of honor. You can also send flowers the day after a party as a thank-you.

IDEAL GIFTS FOR THE HOST

The guest with a gift is always warmly received, and the guest with a really good gift is sure to be invited back. The difference between a dinner-party gift and a gift for an overnight host is really a matter of degree. Wine, for example, works for both: a bottle for a dinner party and a case for a long weekend.

Remember that the presentation is almost as important as the gift itself. Even a simple gift of soap or candles is special when wrapped in an artful way. Make a habit of shopping at places that do beautiful wrapping, or acquire the colorful tissue paper, gift bags, wrapping paper, ribbon—and skills—you need to do the job yourself.

Gifts for dinner and weekend hosts:
- Candles: Two beautiful beeswax tapers, nicely wrapped, for a dinner host, or a large beautifully scented pillar if invited for the weekend
- Basket of seasonal fruit
- Bottle of cognac, port or other after-dinner liqueur
- Bubble bath, soaps and lotions: something for hosts to pamper themselves with after guests have gone. To go all out, combine a selection of toiletries with a pair (or pairs) of pajamas to create a complete relaxation package.
- Slipper and robe set
- Whimsical glasses for the kitchen or bar
- Beautiful coffee-table book of art, design or photography

- Nice bowl or pitcher. Select a plain design that won't clash with your host's décor or include a gift receipt so your host has the option of exchanging it.
- Assortment of rainy-day board games for the family vacation house (see page 94)
- Cozy wool or cashmere blanket or throw for the ski cabin
- New set of beach towels for a summer place
- Monogrammed canvas bag filled with beach reading
- Ice bucket and personalized cocktail napkins
- Small photo album filled with pictures taken during your visit or a nice picture frame with a single photo of you and your hosts

Gifts for a housewarming:
- Linen dishcloths or napkins
- Complete set of guest towels
- Set of glasses
- Pitcher or vase
- Bulbs or seeds for the garden or an attractively potted houseplant
- A selection of local or regional guidebooks
- Membership to a local museum or arts organization

A nice bottle of wine is a fine dinner-party gift, as long as you don't make your host feel that it has to be served immediately. Wrap it up in colored tissue or in a gift bag tied with a ribbon, which will send the clear message that it is a gift to enjoy later. The same goes for food: Unless you've discussed bringing something for the meal with your host, don't present something your host will feel com-pelled to serve right away. Your host already planned the meal and your offering may not go with the menu. If you bring a gift of food, make it something like scones and jam for the next day's breakfast or a box of chocolates or cookies with a note encouraging your host to enjoy them *when the party's over.*

A thank-you gift is mandatory whenever you have been a house-guest. How lavish the gift is depends on the length of your stay and how much your hosts have put them-selves out to entertain you. (You might also consider how much you would have had to spend for a decent hotel room in the area.) You may bring the gift with you—which doesn't get you out of sending a thank-you note after your visit!—or send it once you've returned home. Or you may present something at the end of your stay; a nice way of showing, for example, that you were really paying attention when she admired those vintage linen napkins while you were out shopping together. Another way to thank your hosts is by taking them to dinner during your stay, cooking one of the meals (including shopping and cleanup) or treating them to theater or concert tickets. Make sure to let them know what you're planning in advance so they can schedule their time accordingly.

Note: If your hosts have young children, it's a nice idea to give a small gift to each child. For gift ideas for your hosts, see the sidebar on page 108.

THANK-YOU NOTES

If you've been treated to a sit-down meal or a weekend at someone's home, sending a thank-you note is a must. It doesn't need to be long or formal. It just needs to be sincere and in the mail no more than a couple of days after the party or visit. An invitation to a cocktail party does not require a thank-you note, but a phone call the next day is always appreciated.

Traditionally, a thank-you note is written by one spouse to one of the hosts, thanking both hosts on behalf of both guests. Less formally, you may address your note to both hosts (*Dear Nan and Oliver*)—but sign only your name, since presumably you alone wrote the note. A good thank-you note clearly states that (a) you had a good time, (b) you found something about the event particularly memorable, like a certain dish, the wine or the other guests and (c) you appreciated the invitation and would love to do it again. A good thank-you note is specific and written in a natural voice. Read it aloud; if there's any wording you're not comfortable actually saying, take it out.

An example:

Dear Amanda,

    You and Jonathan gave a beautiful dinner on Saturday. The paella was delicious, and the Spanish wines you chose were the perfect accompaniment. Michael and I thank you for including us, and we look forward to many more happy occasions and meals together.

All the best,
Francesca

When you've been an overnight houseguest, you might write a slightly longer note. Again, say what a great time you (and your spouse and children, if they came along) had during your visit. Second, say something nice about the house or the surrounding area; anything from how comfortable the beds were to how envious you are of the spectacular view from their deck. Mention any specific activities you enjoyed with your hosts, and if you liked their other guests, say so. (And even if you didn't, say you did.) Were your hosts' kids adorable? Say they were, and mention their names and the names of any beloved pets, and you're sure to be invited back. Finally, reiterate how much you appreciated the invitation and be sure to thank each of your hosts by name.

Writing a warm note and sticking a stamp on it shouldn't take you more than five or ten minutes. Make it easy by investing in some nice personalized stationery, if you don't already have it.

Ask the Expert:

THAT'S A WRAP!

When it comes to gifts, "the outside always seems to be more important for me than what's inside," says professional paper-goods fanatic Nancy Laboz, founder and owner of Parcel, a stationery shop in Montclair, New Jersey.

For her personal gift giving, she likes to keep a stockpile of rigid gift boxes with separate lids (known in the trade as set-up boxes) in various shapes and sizes. Since the box itself is attractive, no wrapping paper is necessary—just a pretty ribbon—and you don't have to do any origami-style folding to disguise an oddly shaped gift. They also make great storage for your other wrapping materials. You can buy boxes in bulk from suppliers of paper goods, such as Paper Mart (www.papermart.com), Uline (www.uline.com), or the Box Depot (www.theboxdepot.com). While white is standard, you can order other colors.

Laboz is also a big fan of tags made by hand of unusual materials, such as felt or bridge tally cards, and quirky embellishments like old game pieces and Cracker Jack charms—"anything you can tie on"—that are little keepsakes in themselves. Look for ornaments that relate to the recipient's interests, the gift inside or the holiday being celebrated. Even a simple paper tag can be personalized by rubber-stamping the recipient's initials on it. "Making things lets you be more creative," she says. "Because you're not just buying everything, the gift feels more personal."

You can even use the gift itself as part of the wrapping. "If you're giving a charm necklace," says Laboz, "you could have the necklace inside the box and the charm dangling from the ribbon." This makes the process of opening your gift more of an experience as the whole reveals itself in layers.

When you find a gift-wrapping style that suits you, stock up on the supplies you need and establish your signature look. Think of Tiffany's blue box with its white ribbon, for example. Friends will always know which gift is yours, so no matter what's inside, they'll recognize and appreciate the effort you put into the presentation.

Ask the Expert:
STATIONERY ESSENTIALS

Any note is better than no note, but thank-you notes and other correspondence written on just the right stationery really hit the mark. To build a stationery "wardrobe" for all occasions, start with a folded note, says Megan Kuntze of Crane Stationery. "Because the recipient doesn't see what's written on it right away, it's a little more personal than a correspondence card," says Kuntze.

A flat correspondence card is another essential. More casual in nature than the folded note, it's perfect for sending a quick thank-you to a party host, or for sending an RSVP if no card has been provided. Correspondence cards, like folded notes, can be personalized with your name, monogram, or a personal logo. Stationers make folded notes and correspondence cards in a variety of colors; white or off-white are traditional choices, but nowadays people are increasingly embracing bolder colors, according to Kuntze.

While notes with the words *Thank You* printed on them used to be frowned upon—the logic being that *thank you* should be written in your own hand—Kuntze says, "If it makes it easier for you to send the note, it's worth stocking them as a stationery 'accessory'." And for gift giving, you might consider using your own personalized enclosure card, a small folded note printed or engraved with your monogram or favorite emblem and which comes with its own envelope.

A final piece of the stationery wardrobe, which has been making a comeback of late, is the traditional calling card. More personal than a business card, a personal calling card need contain only as much information as you want to convey to people you meet socially, perhaps just your name and phone number.

Whatever information and decorative elements you choose to include, be sure to coordinate the paper, colors and type styles to create a signature look.

Appendix

SETTING THE TABLE

- Flatware is always arranged in the order of use: The utensils farthest from the plate are used first, and the guests work their way toward the plate as the meal progresses.
- Forks are always placed to the left of each plate, with knives and spoons to the right.
- The lower edges of the utensils should be aligned with the bottom rim of the dinner plate and about one inch from the table edge.
- The blade of the knife (or knives) should always face in toward the plate, not out toward the other diners.
- Fork tines may be placed facing upward, American style, or downward in the Continental style.
- If salad is served as a separate course, a salad fork (and knife, if necessary) is placed in the order of use: to the left of the dinner fork if salad is served first, and to the right of the dinner fork if salad is served after the main course. At a formal dinner, a salad knife, if required, is presented to each diner on a tray.
- A fish fork and knife are placed on the table in order of use.
- At a formal meal with many courses, to reduce clutter, no more than three knives, three forks, and a soup spoon are laid out initially. When additional utensils are needed, they are brought out with the course being served.
- If you are using bread-and-butter plates, they are placed above the forks. The butter spreaders are laid across the bread-and-butter plates

for informal meals and formal luncheons. They may be placed vertically on the right side of the plates, horizontally across the top of the plates or diagonally across the plates. Butter spreaders are not used at a formal dinner in a private home.

- The proper placement of dessert utensils depends on whether the meal is formal or informal. For a formal meal, dessert utensils are presented on each dessert plate, with the fork on the left side and the knife or spoon on the right. For informal affairs, dessert utensils may be set on the table, with the dessert spoon (or knife) placed horizontally above the dinner plate, with the handle facing right and the dessert fork placed beneath the spoon or knife, with the handle facing left or presented on the plate.

- A teaspoon or after-dinner coffee spoon is presented on the saucer, tucked beneath the cup handle, with the handle of the spoon in the four o'clock position.

- The arrangement of stemware depends on space, but, like flatware, generally follows the order of use. Glasses are always placed toward the right (knife) side of the place setting. For a meal with one white and one red wine, a diagonal arrangement of glasses is common, with the white-wine glass in the lower right position, the red-wine glass above and to its left (generally above the spoon) and the water glass in the upper left position, about an inch above the dinner knife.

FOOD: ESTIMATING QUANTITIES

Hors d'oeuvres

With the following estimates, keep in mind the truism that the better the hors d'oeuvres, the more people will want to eat.

- Four to six hors d'oeuvres per person when a meal follows.
- Four to six hors d'oeuvres per person per hour for a cocktail party when no meal follows. For the average two-hour cocktail party, estimate ten to twelve items per person.
- Make three to four servings per person of the more complicated hors d'oeuvres and more of those that are easy to prepare.
- The variety of hors d'oeuvres you offer depends upon the length of your party and the size of your guest list. If it's a long party, plan on offering a wider variety of hors d'oeuvres.

Meals

When doing the math for your next sit-down meal, use common sense, too. If a head of lettuce or broccoli is unusually small, for example, add another.

- Estimate five to six ounces of edible protein (meat, poultry or fish) per person for a main course. Take any bones into account and add weight if necessary. The same goes for a large piece of meat with lots of fat that will melt away during cooking.
- A pound of pasta will serve four to six people for a sit-down dinner or twice as many if part of a buffet.

- Figure one handful of mixed salad per person. One medium head of lettuce should serve about five.
- If you're serving three side dishes (two savory and one sweet) with dinner, allow a half cup of each per person. (If one of your guests is a vegetarian who will be skipping the main course, increase this estimate.)
- For dessert, a 9-inch pie or tart (after a large meal) will serve eight to ten.

THE BAR: ESTIMATING QUANTITIES

Tailor these guidelines to suit the specifics of your party and what you know about the drinking habits of your guests. Remember, it's always better to overestimate your needs than to run out of a party necessity when the party's still in full swing. Unused bottles of wine, for example, can often be returned for a refund.

Drinks

- A standard 750-milliliter bottle of wine yields four to six glasses, depending on who's pouring.
- A 750-milliliter bottle (also called a fifth) of spirits makes about sixteen mixed drinks.
- Expect each guest to have three to four drinks (cocktail, wine, beer or nonalcoholic) during a two- to three-hour cocktail party.
- Assume each adult will drink two to three glasses of wine with dinner, so have at least a half bottle per person.

Ice

If you're serving cocktails, estimate two pounds of ice per person and even more in hot weather. Crushed ice is ideal for chilling wine and beer and for making shaken cocktails, while drinks that are "on the rocks" should be served with ice cubes. Treat your guests to fresh, store-bought ice; homemade ice can absorb freezer odors and impart an odd taste.

Glasses

Allow three glasses per person for a cocktail party. Not everyone will have three drinks, but you want extras for guests who put down their drinks and forget them, or for those who just want a fresh glass. For a seated dinner, two glasses per person for the cocktail hour is enough, plus wine and water glasses for the table.

Cocktail Napkins

Paper is fine for all but the most formal gatherings. When only serving drinks, figure on three napkins per guest, but triple that number if you're serving hors d'oeuvres.

CLASSIC COCKTAILS: STOCKING THE BAR

With the following basics, you can make a bar-worthy repertoire of classic cocktails. Of course, you don't need everything listed here. And it's okay if you can't fill every obscure drink request. With a good bartending manual in hand, figure out which drinks you'd like to serve, note any additional ingredients you may need, like fresh mint for juleps and mojitos, celery and Tabasco sauce for Bloody Marys, then tailor your shopping list accordingly.

Liquor

- Gin, vodka and vermouth (dry and sweet) for martinis, cosmopolitans and more
- Bourbon or rye, and blended whisky for Manhattans, old-fashioneds, whisky sours, highballs, etc.
- Scotch
- Brandy, a key ingredient in classic cocktails like the brandy Alexander, sidecar and Singapore sling
- Rum for Cuba libres, mojitos and more
- Cognac or port for after-dinner sipping
- Tequila, because who doesn't love a margarita?
- Cointreau or triple sec for that hint of orange flavor in a cosmopolitan or a margarita

Mixers and Garnishes

- Lemons, limes and oranges for juice, peel and garnishes
- Club soda and tonic water. Smaller bottles or cans ensure it will be fresh and fizzy for each drink.
- Ginger ale and cola
- Maraschino cherries
- Pitted olives and cocktail onions
- Juice, including orange, cranberry, lemon, grapefruit and tomato
- Superfine sugar and simple syrup (sugar that's been dissolved in boiling water and allowed to cool)
- Coarse salt
- Bitters

COCKTAIL PARTY SHOPPING LIST

Décor

- Flowers
- Candles

Bar

(see also Classic Cocktails, page 124)

- Liquor: vodka, gin, dry vermouth, blended whisky and Scotch
- Wine
- Beer
- Nonalcoholic beverages: juices, soft drinks and sparkling water
- Mixers and garnishes: soda and tonic water, lemons, limes and olives

Food

- Assorted hors d'oeuvres: four to six per person per hour

Miscellaneous

- Cocktail napkins
- Ice

Consider renting

- Glassware
- Ice buckets
- Garbage cans
- Coatracks and hangers

DINNER PARTY SHOPPING LIST

Décor

- Flowers
- Centerpiece
- Candles: for the table and other areas of the house
- Holiday decorations

Food

- Nuts, olives or other salty snacks for cocktails
- Hors d'oeuvres (optional)— four to six per person
- Appetizer
- Main course
- Side dishes
- Salad
- Dessert

Beverages

- Wine: half bottle per person for the meal, plus extra for before-dinner drinks

- Liquor, mixers, ice and lemons or limes for cocktail garnishes (optional)
- Nonalcoholic beverages, including juices like orange, grapefruit and cranberry
- Coffee, milk and cream or half-and-half
- After-dinner drinks (optional)

Miscellaneous

- Place cards
- Menu cards

Consider renting

- Plates and serving platters
- Flatware
- Glassware
- Linens

HOW TO DECANT A BOTTLE OF WINE

Decanting, pouring wine from its original bottle into a special glass decanter before serving, is an elegant way to enhance the enjoyment of a fine wine. White wines, however, poured into wineglasses are generally ready to drink right from the bottle. Reds, though, may benefit from having some time to "open up," and older vintages are often decanted to remove the sediment (grape solids) that accumulates in a bottle over time. Simply opening up a bottle of wine without decanting it is not enough to allow it to "breathe" as only about one inch of the wine will be exposed to air.

Make sure you start with a scrupulously clean and dry decanter. If you want to impress guests, use the restaurant sommelier's trick of holding the bottle a few inches above a candle while you pour the wine into the decanter. The light from the candle allows you to see when you get to any sediment left floating at the bottom of the bottle. Pour in one uninterrupted motion until you see the first sign of sediment. Stop pouring there. With an older wine, you may need to leave about 10 percent in the bottle, but the 90 percent you have left to drink will be absolutely clean and free of sediment.

Older wines should be drunk soon after they're uncorked. Once exposed to air, they begin to decompose quickly. Newer wines, though, can benefit from thirty minutes or so of "breathing" at room temperature.

HOW TO OPEN A BOTTLE OF CHAMPAGNE

To open a Champagne bottle, first remove the metal foil covering. Then, with your hand firmly over the cork, twist off and remove the wire bonnet holding the cork. Place a kitchen towel or cloth napkin over the top of the cork and hold the bottle at a 45 degree angle, aiming away from people, glasses and windows. With your hand still grasping the cork through the napkin, carefully remove the cork by twisting the bottle (not the cork) a quarter turn or so until you begin to feel the cork loosen. Then gently ease the cork out, turning the bottle a little more if needed. When the cork is released, you will hear a gentle pop. Try to avoid making a noisy pop, which encourages the escape of air and disperses the bubbles. And don't ever remove just the wire bonnet and leave the cork in the bottle. The pressure will build inside the bottle, and the unattended cork may pop out on its own. Champagne should always be served very cold. Once opened, keep the bottle in an ice bucket filled with ice and water (the water is important, because that's what conducts the cold).

PREPARING YOUR HOME: THE PARTY TO-DO LIST

One to Two Weeks Before

- Evaluate your space. Make sure you have enough tables and chairs. Note any furniture that needs to be moved before the party.
- Plan the decorations, deciding on a theme or a color scheme. If you are using a professional florist, consult her on the price and availability of flowers to fit your theme.
- For a dinner party, plan your table settings and centerpieces. Make sure you have enough dishes, flatware and glassware. If not, consider buying replacements or renting your tableware.
- Check your tablecloths and cloth napkins for stains or holes; wash and iron if necessary.

Two Days Before

- Thoroughly clean house and rearrange furniture if needed. This way, on the day of the party you'll only have minor touch-ups to do.

The Day Before

- Pick up flowers or have them delivered so they have time to open up before the party.
- For a cocktail party, set up your bar area. Put out liquor, mixers, bar tools, glassware and anything else that doesn't need to be kept cold. Put white wine and Champagne in the refrigerator to chill.
- For a dinner party, arrange the table centerpiece and set the table. Lay out dishes, cups and utensils for dessert, too.
- Select your party music and have it ready to go.
- Place candles where you want them around the house.

The Day of the Party

- Walk through the house and spot-clean as necessary. Fluff sofa pillows and put away anything valuable or breakable.
- Assemble your serving platters.
- Sweep the front walk and turn on outside lights.
- Put out flowers.
- Shortly before guests arrive, step outside for a minute. When you come back in, note any odors, then use a room spray or light a scented candle in trouble areas.
- Light candles and start a fire in the fireplace, in season.
- Turn on music.
- Set out appetizers.

PREPARING FOR AN OVERNIGHT GUEST: TO-DO LIST

One to Two Weeks Before

- Call or e-mail to confirm details of the visit with your guest(s). Send directions by mail or e-mail.
- Spend time in the proposed guest room, noting anything that's missing. Clear space for guests' clothing in closets and dressers.
- Take stock of your guest sheets and towels; wash and iron.
- Plan menus, shop and prepare a few dishes in advance, if possible.
- Think about activities for your guests. Start compiling information on local attractions, transportation schedules and entertainment listings.

One to Two Days Before

- Thoroughly clean the guest bedroom and bathroom.
- Make the bed.
- Put out fresh towels.
- Empty wastebaskets.

The Day of Arrival

- Place flowers in the guest room, plus a fresh pitcher of water with glasses.
- Hang a clean bathrobe in the closet.

Guest Bedroom Essentials

- Bed (or makeshift bed) made up with clean sheets and pillowcases (ironed, for a special touch)
- Season-appropriate blanket or comforter with an extra blanket folded at the foot of the bed
- Bedside table with good reading light and box of tissues
- Closet space or clothes butler with a few good, preferably wooden, hangers
- Drawer space in a dresser or bureau or, if no drawers are available, a suitcase stand
- Working clock or clock radio with an alarm
- Wastebasket
- Nightlight

Guest Bedroom Extras

- Vase of fresh flowers
- Pitcher of water (refilled nightly) and a clean glass or two
- Books and magazines. Your guests might decide to read quietly in bed instead of staying up in the living room with the TV on.
- An extra pillow for each guest to make sleeping or reading in bed more comfortable
- Stationery (with stamps), and pens
- Fresh robe and slippers
- Television
- CD player

Guest Bathroom Essentials

- Fresh bar of soap
- Fresh roll of toilet paper, plus a backup roll
- Clean matching bath towels, hand towels and washcloths. If you're hosting several guests, assign a different color to each person to eliminate any confusion.
- Bath mat

Guest Bathroom Extras

- Toothpaste and toothbrush (in the original wrapper)
- Shampoo and conditioner
- Bath salts or oils
- Body and hand lotions
- Disposable razor and shaving cream
- Sponge and bathroom cleaner so a thoughtful guest can clean up after himself
- Scented candle
- Air freshener
- Dental floss and mouthwash
- Cotton balls and cotton swabs
- Nail file and clippers
- Aspirin and ibuprofin
- Adhesive bandages and antibiotic ointment

GREAT PARTY MUSIC

Music can breathe life into your next party. Team up some of your personal favorites with some of the suggestions here and tailor the tunes to suit the occasion and the crowd. For dinner music, think soft and instrumental. Cocktail tunes can be livelier but not so loud that the music makes conversation difficult. A professional DJ's trick: if you really want to liven things up, create a mix of hits from the era when most of your guests were at their wildest, which is usually their college years.

Some crowd-pleasing suggestions for a range of occasions:

- Dexter Gordon, *Our Man in Paris*. Jazz ballads and swinging be-bop from a master of the tenor saxophone.
- Frank Sinatra, *Songs for Swingin' Lovers*. One of Sinatra's most highly acclaimed albums, includes the definitive recordings of "I've Got You under My Skin," "Anything Goes," and "Pennies from Heaven."
- Patricia Barber, *Nightclub*. Spare, sophisticated interpretations of jazz standards by a contemporary pianist/singer.
- Miles Davis, *Kind of Blue*. Cool, mysterious, and masterful. If you own only one jazz album, make it this one.
- Antonio Carlos Jobim and Elis Regina, *Elis & Tom*. A powerful singer (Regina) and one of Brazil's greatest songwriters (Jobim) team up with timeless results on this bossa nova standard.
- Stan Getz, João Gilberto, *Getz/Gilberto*. This collaboration between the great American saxophonist Getz and Brazilian composer/guitarist Gilberto is the other bossa nova album that belongs in everyone's

music library. "Corcovado" and "Girl From Ipanema" (sung by Gilberto's wife, Astrud) are among the highlights.

- Al Green, *Greatest Hits*. Soulful, sexy R&B, including "Let's Stay Together" and "Tired of Being Alone."
- Various Artists, *The Very Best of Cole Porter*. Yes, one man wrote all those songs, including "It's De-Lovely," "I Get a Kick out of You," and "Night and Day." The performers on this album, including Tony Bennett, Ella Fitzgerald, Dinah Washington and Mel Torme, put these songs over the top.
- Buena Vista Social Club, *Buena Vista Social Club*. An irresistible survey of Cuban musical styles of the pre-Castro era.
- Cesaria Evora, *Cabo Verde*. Evora's rich voice and the syncopated rhythms of her acoustic backing band create a haunting, intoxicating sound. An unusual pick that your guests will love.

BIBLIOGRAPHY

Baldrige, Letitia. *New Manners for New Times: A Complete Guide to Etiquette*. New York: Scribner, 2003.

Blumer, Bob. "High and Dry." www.salon.com/april97/food/surreal970409.html.

Collins, Philip. *The Art of the Cocktail: 100 Classic Cocktail Recipes*. San Francisco: Chronicle Books, 1992.

Editors of *Esquire* magazine. *Esquire's Handbook for Hosts: A Time-Honored Guide to the Perfect Party*. New York: Black Dog & Leventhal Publishers, 1999 (originally published 1949).

Graham, Katharine. *Personal History*. New York: Vintage Books, 1997.

Hess, Robert. "The Perfect Martini." www.drinkboy.com.

LaFerla, Ruth. "Unearthing the Notebook That Unnerved Society." *New York Times*, November 25, 2001.

Maroukian, Francine. *Town & Country Elegant Entertaining*. New York: Hearst Books, 2004.

Nebens, Amy. *A Gracious Welcome: Etiquette and Ideas for Entertaining Houseguests*. San Francisco: Chronicle Books, 2004.

Plimpton, George. *Truman Capote: In Which His Friends, Enemies, Acquaintances, and Various Detractors Recall His Turbulent Career*. New York: Nan A. Talese, 1997.

Post, Peggy. *Emily Post's Etiquette, 17th Edition: The Definitive Guide to Manners, Completely Revised and Updated*. New York: HarperResource, 2004.

Post, Peggy. *Entertaining: A Classic Guide to Adding Elegance and Ease to Any Festive Occasion*. New York: HarperResource, 1998.

Smith, Sally Bedell. *Grace and Power: The Private World of the Kennedy White House*. New York: Random House, 2004.

Spade, Kate. *Occasions*. New York: Simon & Schuster, 2004.

St. John, Warren. "The Five-Decade Book Party and Its Tireless Host." *New York Times*, October 5, 2003.

von Drachenfels, Suzanne. *The Art of the Table*. New York: Simon & Schuster, 2000.

Zellerbach, Merla. "Pat Montandon: From Party Girl to Peacenik." *Nob Hill Gazette*. Reprinted at http://patmontandon.com.

INDEX

A

activities, for overnight guests, 92–95, 104–105

argumentative guests, 65–66

awkward situations, 62–66
    argumentative guests, 65–66
    guests breaking something, 64–65, 103
    guests refusing to leave, 63–64
    intoxicated guests, 63
    unexpected guests, 62, 100

B

bar. *See also* champagne; wine
    accessories, 38–39
    alternatives, 36–38
    cocktail napkins, 123
    estimating quantities, 122–123
    glasses, 39, 43–44, 123
    ice for, 39, 122
    intoxicated guests and, 63
    liquor, 36–38, 122, 124
    martini recipe, 37
    mixers/garnishes, 125
    shopping lists, 126, 127
    stocking, 124–125

bartending
    hiring professionals, 42–43
    yourself, 38–39

bathroom
    for overnight guests, 134
    party preparation, 23

beverages. *See* bar; champagne; wine

boss, dinner party for, 61

broken articles, 64–65, 103

buffet(s)
    basics, 16–17
    food, 30–31
    lighting, 22
    seated, 79–80
    service, 79–80

C

canceling events, 72–73

candles, 21–22, 26–27, 108

caterers, 40–42

centerpieces, 26, 49

champagne
    opening, 129
    serving, 35

children
    gifts for, 111
    as overnight guests, 90–91
    parties and, 74, 100

china, 24, 43
cleaning up, after parties, 83, 84–85
cocktail parties
  basics of, 15
  shopping list, 126
conversations
  encouraging, 57–60
  handling argumentative guests,
    65–66
  jump-starters for, 59
  participating in (as guest), 101
country clubs, parties at, 44–46

D

dietary restrictions, 33, 101
dinner parties
  basics of, 16
  for bosses, 61
  cleaning up after, 83, 84–85
  food dishes, 31–32
  gifts for hosts, 107–111
  serving food, 75–76
  shopping list, 127
dishes. *See* table settings

F

flowers
  as host gifts, 107
  for parties, 23, 48–49
food
  for buffets, 30–31
  caterers, 40–42
  estimating quantities, 120–121
  hors d'oeuvres, 29–30, 120

as host gift, 110
for overnight guests, 91–92
party shopping lists, 126, 127
restricted diets, 33, 101
serving, 74–80
for sit-down dinners, 31–32
formal meals. *See* dinner parties

G

gifts, for hosts
  dinner/weekend events, 108–109,
    110
  before event, 107
  housewarming gifts, 109
  ideas for, 107–111
  overnight stays and, 110–111
  wrapping, 113–114
glasses
  for bar, 39, 43–44, 123
  cleaning, 84–85
  renting, 43–44, 126, 127
greeting guests. *See* welcoming guests
guest bathroom, 134
guest bedroom, 89–90, 133
guest etiquette, 99–115
  gifts for hosts, 107–111
  overnight stays, 102–107
  parties, 100–102
  thank-you notes, 111–112,
    114–115
guest(s). *See also* overnight guests
  argumentative, 65–66
  awkward situations with, 62–66
  breaking something, 64–65

encouraging conversations among,
57–60

etiquette of. *See* guest etiquette

of honor, 60, 107

intoxicated, 63

introducing, 53–55

lists, 17–18

refusing to leave, 63–64

unexpected, 62, 100

welcoming, 19–21, 52–53

H

home preparation
for overnight guests, 88, 132–133
for parties, 18–23, 130–131

hors d'oeuvres, 29–30, 120

house guests. *See* overnight guests

housewarming gifts, 109

I

ice, 39, 122

informal meals, serving, 77–78

intoxicated guests, 63

introducing guests, 53–55

invitations, 66–69
accepting, 100
adults only and, 74
appropriateness of, 66–67
calling guest before sending, 67
information on, 68–69
lead times for, 68
RSVPs, 69, 74, 100
thanking host for, 102
types of, 66–67

K

Kennedy White House, 25

kids. *See* children

L

leaving parties, 63–64, 102

lighting, 21–22

linens
as host gifts, 108, 109
for overnight guests, 106–107
renting, 43, 127
table settings, 24–26

liquor. *See* bar

M

martini recipe, 37

meals. *See* dinner parties; food

menu cards, 28

mingling/conversations, 57–60

music
lighting and, 21–22
playing/mood of, 21
suggested tunes, 135–136

N

names
forgetting/recovering, 55–57
remembering, 56

napkins
cocktail, 123
table settings and, 26

O

outings, for overnight guests, 92–95
overnight guests
    accommodations for, 89–90, 133
    activities for, 92–95
    checklist for, 132–133
    etiquette of, 102–107
    expert advice on, 96–97
    food for, 91–92
    four-star service, 96–97
    gifts from, 107–111, 113–114
    preparing for, 88, 132–133
    rainy-day games for, 94
    saying good-bye, 95
    thank-you notes from, 112, 114–115
    welcoming, 89

P

parties. *See also* buffet(s); cocktail parties; dinner parties; guest etiquette; guest(s)
    in apartments, 20
    awkward situations at, 62–66
    beverages for. *See* bar; champagne; wine
    canceling, 72–73
    categories of, 15–17
    children and, 74, 100
    cleaning up after, 83, 84–85
    at country clubs, 44–46
    encouraging conversations, 57–60
    forgetting/remembering names, 55–57

    gifts for hosts, 107–111, 113–114
    guests of honor, 60, 107
    invitations for. *See* invitations
    kids and, 74
    lighting for, 21–22
    making introductions, 53–55
    making toasts, 71–72
    music for, 21, 135–136
    pets and, 74
    reciprocating hospitality, 102
    at restaurants, 44–46
    seating arrangements, 70–71
    shopping lists, 126–127
    surprise, 73
    thank-you notes, 111–112
    welcoming guests, 19–21, 52–53
    at the White House, 25
party preparation. *See also* bar; food
    in apartments, 20
    defining party type and, 14–17
    guest lists, 17–18
    hiring professionals, 40–43
    home preparation, 18–23, 130–131
    for restaurant/country club parties, 44–46
    table settings, 24–28
pets, 74, 88, 104
place cards, 27–28

R

rainy-day games, 94
remembering names, 56
rentals, 43–44, 126, 127
restaurants, parties at, 44–46

restricted diets, 33, 101
RSVPs, 69, 74, 100

S

seating arrangements, 70–71
serving
    buffet meals, 79–80
    champagne, 35
    cleaning up after, 83, 84–85
    food, 74–80
    formal meals, 75–76
    informal meals, 77–78
    wine, 80–82
setting table. *See* table settings
smoking, 101
stationery essentials, 114–115
surprise parties, 73

T

table settings, 24–28. *See also* glasses
    broken dinnerware and, 64–65
    candles/centerpieces, 26–27, 49
    clearing/cleaning up, 83, 84–85
    linens/china/silver/glassware,
      24–26, 43
    menu cards, 28
    place cards, 27–28
    setting table, 118–119

temperature, in house, 22
thank-you gifts, 110–111
thank-you notes, 111–112, 114–115
toasts, making, 71–72

U

unexpected guests, 62, 100

V

vegetarian/vegan meals, 33

W

welcoming guests
    for overnight stays, 89
    for parties, 19–21, 52–53
White House parties, 25
wine. *See also* champagne
    decanting, 128
    estimating quantities, 36
    expert advice on, 47–48
    as host gift, 108, 110
    serving, 80–82
    temperature, 80
    uncorking, 81
    what to serve, 34–36, 48–49
wrapping gifts, 113–114